Pathways to Tremendous Success - Weekly Devotional

SUCCESS DEVOTIONAL

Published by: Chistell Publishing
                     7235 Aventine Way, Suite #201
                     Chattanooga, TN 37421

                     ISBN: 978-0-9663539-8-3

"There is no better time to start designing a remarkable life for yourself than <u>right now</u>."

Pathways to Tremendous Success - Weekly Devotional

Congratulations on making the decision to take your life forward. Starting now, you can make decisions and take smart actions that lead to tremendous success. Your past can't stop you, not if you're ready to move forward.

Be prepared to examine your life and focus on living with clarity. That shared, getting to the life that you want isn't magic. It's an ongoing process that can payoff tremendously and in surprisingly good ways.

Key life areas, *including* relationship improvements, mindfulness, pattern breaking, vision and commitment are explored within <u>Pathways to Tremendous Success</u>. The book is broken down into one weekly focus area.

You don't have to read the book in chronological order. In fact, you can benefit from reading <u>Pathways to</u> <u>Tremendous Success</u> whether you read a chapter of the book one week at a time or simply turn to any page in the book and start reading.

However, the book's full advantage may not be achieved until you read *all of the book*. Additionally, *actually practicing* techniques shared in <u>Pathways to Tremendous Success</u> may yield long-term results.

Don't just read <u>Pathways to Tremendous Success</u>. Take advantage of the worksheets, filling them out as you examine your life. Above all, trust the Creator and believe in your innate good.

At the end of the book and after you've completed the worksheets, don't be surprised if your life has changed. Yet, it's not magic. That shared, the techniques in <u>Pathways to Tremendous Success</u> are relatively easy to implement.

You're to be commended for getting started. Here's to your marvelous, remarkable life.

TABLE OF CONTENTS

TABLE OF CONTENTS

Dedication

SUCCESS DEVOTIONAL

For my son.

I love you, Gregory –

Week 1
Identify and Remember Your Primary Goal

Your primary goal takes precedence over all other aims that you have. This goal will remain unchanged throughout your physical experience. Set a goal that aligns with your core values and your core beliefs.

As an example, my primary goal is to awaken and be one with Source. Every other aim that I pursue, from writing novels and non-fiction books to sharing educational and motivational insights via public speaking, remains within the scope of my primary goal. It impacts what I write and publish, say and do.

If you're like me, you may see your sub-goals (goals beneath your primary goal) change. Experiences, life adjustments and resource shifts could find you resetting or altering any or all of your other goals. But, your primary goal should remain unchanged. It works like a driver.

Consider praying and asking Source what your primary goal is. Another way to state this is to ask what *your purpose for being in the world is*. Other techniques that you could use to discover your primary goal are to meditate, spend time in nature, get enough sleep to allow messages from your preconscious to surface into your conscious mind via a dream, prompting or a vision. Also, stay flexible and engage in your passions (these are activities that cause you to experience peace and joy). The longer you do what you love, the more you could stir up an "aha!" moment from within yourself.

Take your time with this. Give yourself at least a week to consider what your primary goal is. You may be surprised at how your primary goal serves as an anchor over the course of your physical experience.

For example, Jesus, the Christ, knew what his primary goal in this world was. He never forgot his primary goal. He never let any other experience turn him away from that primary goal. As a tip, whatever your primary goal is, make sure that it is rooted in love.

"So whether you eat or drink or whatever you do, do it all for the glory of God."
1 Corinthians 10:31

Write Down Your Primary Goal – Get Specific

_____

_____

_____

_____

_____

_____

_____

_____

_____

_____

Week 2
Gaining Clarity

It's critical that you gain clarity about your value, your limitless worth. You need to know that your value will never be altered. Furthermore, you need to know that your value is beyond words. You are priceless. It's also important that you get clear about what you want and why you want what you want.

Although it may have escaped your awareness, your entire life, you have been doing this. You have been allowing yourself to *only* receive the good that you believe you deserve. The value that *you place on yourself* influences *everything* in your life – *everything*.

So, get clear about your worth. Don't rush this process. If you do, you could find yourself revisiting this decades from now, after you have experienced challenges.

To gain clarity about your value, read scriptures that focus on what the Creator says about you. Observe how nature serves you with water, food, air and wonder. Consider that your value is limitless. Actually sit still and consider this.

To gain clarity about a goal that you're interested in pursuing, write down what you want to gain guidance about. Be specific. For example, if you're interested in operating a downtown café and want to know what to do to achieve the goal, write that at the top of a blank sheet of paper.

Sit still for 5 to 10 minutes in the morning and again for 5 to 10 minutes at night. Look at what you wrote that you want to gain guidance about. Then, sit still and become aware of thoughts that surface. Do this for several days, until clear guidance reaches your conscious mind.

Regarding the goal to operate a downtown café, ideas to conduct market research on the best locations to operate a restaurant, rates for top cooks and where to find bamboo furniture might surface. Later, you could get ideas related to lunch menu food items and short order food pricing.

As a tip, a spiral notebook might be best, as a myriad of thoughts could surface during this process. You can also use this book to write down ideas that pop into your mind. The important thing is to get these thoughts down as they could prove helpful over the coming days, weeks and years.

"Clarity invites passion, purpose and empowerment into your life."

Author Denise Turney

Write Down Your Ideas – Get Specific, Be Clear

_____

_____

_____

_____

_____

_____

_____

_____

_____

_____

_____

Week 3
Practice Appreciation

Appreciation is sun rays in a good life. When I was a kid, my paternal grandmother encouraged me to practice appreciation. "Be grateful," she'd tell me. Years later, I would learn that practicing appreciation is a way to *focus* on the good in life.

Fortunately, I did practice appreciation. But, I started to add beliefs to it that would later leave me feeling less than good. Those beliefs came through religious routines. Before long, instead of feeling *sincere* appreciation, I started to feel as if I *had* to be grateful. On top of that, I told myself that if I didn't express gratitude, God would take things I liked away from me, as if punishing me.

What was the outcome?

Instead of waking with appreciation, I started waking up thinking "do I have to do this all over again". Life itself, for me, started to feel like running on a hamster wheel. Each day started to hold similar experiences. Repeating life experiences day after day is not a way to experience appreciation, at least not for me.

At the worst, after years of not practicing appreciation, I entered a period where I didn't hear birds signing and I could swear that I not once saw a butterfly. Then, one day, I lifted my hands and called out "thank you" to Source. What a good experience!

That was about 15 years ago. Ever since, I have raised my hands and said, "thank you" as soon as I waken and get out of bed. I am committed to practicing *sincere* appreciation. Goodness knows what hardships that one appreciation practice has kept me away from. I can only imagine the blessings that practicing appreciation has brought and continues to bring into my life.

Here are some ways that you could practice appreciation each day:

- Write down five blessings that you've experienced in a journal. Use your laptop or computer if you're interested in saving time. Just remember that writing may stimulate the parietal lobe in the brain. Keep your appreciation journals. They can prove beneficial years later, especially should you go through a challenge.

- Lift your hands in the morning and at night and say "thank you". Simply say "thank you".

See if this doesn't leave you feeling better than waking and saying something like "do I have to do this again?" Or "ugh, another trying day".

- Engage in at least three daily activities that you enjoy. These are activities that find you feeling warm, happy, cared for and valued.
- Get outdoors in nature. You might be surprised at how being outdoors in natural sunlight balances and shifts your mood.
- Write an appreciation letter to people who fill your life with goodness.
- Create a poem about a hobby, talent or skill that you love and appreciate engaging in.

"Do not be anxious about anything, but in every situation, by prayer and petition, with thanksgiving, present your requests to God."
Philippians 4:6

What Do You Sincerely Appreciate – Write It Down

_____

_____

_____

_____

_____

_____

_____

_____

_____

_____

Week 4
Bless Yourself with Sufficient Rest

Sleep and restful living are keys to staying on course. Ask any of the approximately 1 in 4 Americans who suffer with insomnia how important a good night sleep is.

According to Med Alert Help, adults need between 7 to 9 hours of sleep a night. What you might find surprising is that each part of your body undergoes change while you sleep.[1]

It sounds good. Yet, how something sounds and how it evolves isn't always, if ever, the same. Fortunately, there's help. There are choices that you can make to improve your sleep.

To begin, wind down an hour before you head to bed. Try it. Actually sit down and read a relaxing book or watch a relaxing movie before you head to bed. Allow your body time to unwind. Also, avoid caffeine and starchy food.

Regarding diet, you might find it beneficial to eat a few cherries or to drink a cherry beverage before you go to bed. Cherries contain natural melatonin.

Other steps that you could take to encourage better sleep include:

- Meditating for 5 to 10 minutes before you retire for the night.
- Respond to important emails and phone messages before you start to relax for the evening. The point is to clear your mind of projects that you're working on.
- Avoid drinking too much water to prevent yourself from waking in the middle of the night with a full bladder.
- Write down concerns that you have, as well as steps that you may take to resolve those concerns. This step can clear your mind.
- Go to bed around the same time each night. Doing so could train your brain to start to prepare for sleep.
- Write down your dreams. This can encourage sleep, seeing the reward of a guiding or insightful dream as part of the sleep process.

"It's impossible to put a price on a good night of sleep. Ask a wealthy person with insomnia. She knows."
Author Denise Turney

Resources

1. 48 Surprising Sleep Statistics & Facts to Know in 2021 (medalerthelp.org)

Write Down Dreams & Blessings You've Experienced Due to Good Sleep

_____

_____

_____

_____

_____

_____

_____

_____

_____

Week 5
Express Yourself

Your true self wants to be felt and heard. Despite feedback that you might receive from others, comments that might tempt you to try to be invisible, you didn't enter this world to hide. On the contrary, you came here to express yourself, to showcase what you truly are.

Here's good news. It's not necessary for you to be an artist to express yourself. Singing around your home or while you're outside is one way that you could express yourself. And, check this out. This is a self-expression act that I recently tried. See how it feels.

It's easy. Simply put on one of your favorite songs and start dancing. Actually dance. Keep dancing until you reach the end of the song. You can do this while you're alone or among a safe group of people in a safe environment. Did I ever feel energetic, alive and alert while I danced! Sure. At the start, judgmental thoughts rose up within me. But, I kept dancing.

That's the blessing of self-expression. The more that you express your sincere self, the more you may find yourself pushing beyond inner and external judgements and criticism. Additionally, you might feel better because you'll be letting more parts of you be heard. If you've ever done parts work, you know how one or more parts of you could start to feel stifled or muffled. By expressing your true self, you can step away from these negative experiences.

Looking for more ways to engage in self-expression?

Try journaling. Working with an adult coloring book is another way that you could make expressing yourself part of your daily routine.

Building crafts, playing a musical instrument and writing poems are other ways that you can express yourself. Writing a play or novel are other ways. The aim is to let all parts of you be heard and expressed.

"Sincere self-expression is your life's beautiful artwork."

Author Denise Turney

Write Down How You're Expressing Your True Self

_____

_____

_____

_____

_____

_____

_____

_____

_____

_____

Week 6
Fall in Love with Movement

Exercise, dance or ride a bike. There are so many fun ways to add movement to your life! Dance to your favorite song just once and you may experience the rewards of body movement. It's freeing, empowering and creative. You might not think about it, but a lot of movement taps into your personal creativity. Among all movements, dance may do this most.

Not in love with dancing? Here are more ways to have fun moving your body. Relax into 30 minutes of yoga. Years ago, I did yoga as a way to relax and visualize running smoothly to the point that I broke my best cross-country and track and field records. Will always remember the time when I was doing yoga and got so relaxed that I fell over limp, as if there were no bones in my body. That's when I knew that yoga worked.

Start out small with yoga if you're new to this type of body movement. There are yoga instruction videos that you can use to help guide your movements or to give you creative ideas to incorporate into your yoga practices. Swimming, including water dancing, hiking, stair stepping, skipping, rock climbing and rope jumping are other ways to move your body.

Back to dance, you could tap dance, perform ballet or do upper body dance movements. The latter might work well if you're currently limited to a chair. No worries if you have negative perceptions around body movement or exercising.

To evolve your perceptions around exercise, consider teaming up with a friend. If you've ever enjoyed discussing a recent experience that you've been worrying about with a friend while you were walking, you may well know how good it feels to move with a friend.

You'll also be burning calories and toning your tendons, not to mention strengthening your cardiovascular system. More benefits of moving your body range from an improved mood to a strong muscular system to healthier self-esteem. If you move your body outdoors, the vitamin D could strengthen your bones and allow your body to heal faster.

This next benefit may be a surprising side effect of exercising. The more that you move (without over-doing it), the higher your energy levels may rise.

Check out these additional benefits associated with moving your body:

- Lower blood pressure – Walking in nature has been shown to reduce stress hormones. This, in turn, could (even if only temporarily) lower blood pressure.
- Help ward off depression – This is another benefit that I learned firsthand. Walking or running outdoors in nature for 40 minutes can shift your mood. Over time, moving your body outdoors for 40 consecutive minutes could ward off depression. This is because exercise may improve blood flow. It can also help with the release of endorphins.
- Flexibility – As you move your body in healthy ways, you may experience less stiffness and joint pain. This is because exercise helps to reduce cortisol levels, reducing inflammation.

If you're impacted by the amount of sunlight that you receive daily, just one year of dealing with seasonal affective disorder (SAD) may be enough to point you toward more outdoor body movement. If you're someone who experiences mood shifts during the start or end of Autumn, you might want to consider exercising outdoors for 40 consecutive minutes three or more times a week.

Howbeit, if you're free of SAD, you may love the rewards gained from moving your body regularly. Looking to start small? During the daytime, park further away from the office or shopping center. Do this if it'll still be light when you exit the building and return to your car.

Also, consider taking the stairs instead of an elevator. The point is to get moving, particularly outdoors. Take a friend with you or enjoy exercising on your own. Just get moving in safe, healthy ways. It's a good idea to add a morning and evening stretch to your body movement routine, especially as you age. Stretching may help eliminate stiffness and improve balance.

"Even when all is known, the care of a man is not yet complete, because eating alone will not keep a man well; he must also take exercise. For food and exercise, while possessing opposite qualities, yet work together to produce health."

Hippocrates

How Are You Going to Add Movement to Your Day?

_____

_____

_____

_____

_____

_____

_____

_____

_____

_____

_____

Week 7
Feed Your Body Good Health

Similar to a relationship that you don't appreciate until it's over, it's been said that you don't *really* appreciate your good health until it's gone. Yet, you don't have to wait until you're facing a mountain of declining health to start making better food and beverage choices. To make it easier, think about starting small.

This may prove to be especially effective if yours has been a diet of sugary foods and beverages. Or, you might have been feeding yourself a diet heavy in processed foods like potato chips, processed microwavable dinners, pizza, processed meat, muffins, cookies and white rice. Instead of trying to eliminate all sugary and processed food from your diet, consider replacing one sugary food with a fresh, green leafy vegetable.

Another choice that you could take is to replace soda or sugary juices with a glass of fresh water. Just start small. And, rather than completely letting go of a food or beverage, often replace it with a healthier food or beverage. That way, your diet can stay full, interesting, colorful and exciting.

Whether you've decided to start making the healthier switch now or prefer to take that on later, check out the below healthy foods that you could pump your health up with:

- Kale – You might love eating raw rainbow kale in the morning.
- Collard greens – They are easy and quick to cook and taste delicious, especially when seasoned with white vinegar and ingredients like garlic, shallots, cabbage and chicken broth.
- Spinach – Another food that you could eat raw or in a salad
- Brown Rice – Serves as a great foundation food to top with steamed vegetables
- Cabbage
- Salmon
- Cherries
- Apples
- Blueberries
- Strawberries
- Almonds
- Macadamia nuts – Get these from Hawaii and you may come to love these nuts
- Broccoli – This healthy food works well in salad and in soup.
- Shrimp
- Green beans
- Onions
- Carrots

- Fresh water – This one is hard to beat, especially when you consider how it aids in flushing pollutants out of the body.
- Vegetable juice – Consider making a healthy vegetable juice at home. All you need is a good blender. You might even prefer to drink a glass of home blended vegetable juice versus eating a sausage, egg and cheese muffin for breakfast.
- Fruit juice – Similar to vegetable juice, you could blend your own fruits into a juice drink.
- Herbal tea – Guava, graviola and lemon herbal are just a few herbal teas that you could add to your diet. In addition to providing a smooth, easy texture, herbal teas could help you to relax.

This is just a start. If you ask your relatives and friends who love to cook to share their favorite healthy foods and recipes, your list of choices will expand. Clearly, enjoying a healthy diet doesn't have to be boring. So, get creative. Your body may thank you for feeding it good for years to come.

"The doctor of the future will no longer treat the human frame with drugs, but rather will cure and prevent disease with nutrition."

Thomas Edison

What Healthy Foods and Drinks Are You Spicing Up Your Diet with (Remember to replace one unhealthy food or drink with a healthy one)

_____

_____

_____

_____

_____

_____

_____

_____

_____

_____

Week 8
Where Reading Fits In

Reading good books does more than ignite imagination. Reading good books stimulates creativity, provides motivation, inspiration, instruction and empowerment. Curl up on the sofa, an outdoor porch step or on a warm bed with a good book and start delving into the heart of a story and you might feel the type of deep connection that you've been seeking for months.

It is through reading good books that you can feel less alone in the world. Did I ever learn this first hand. When I was a kid, I read dozens of books a week. Favorites of mine were Pippi Longstocking stories, Judy Blume book series and later Mildred Taylor, Maya Angelou, Richard Wright and Gwendolyn Brooks. These books ranged from children's books to middle school to adult fiction, including poetry, short stories and full length novels.

Admittedly, my initial reason for reading was simply to be entertained. Entertainment still remains a major reason why I buy and read books. Howbeit, from my early days of reading, books helped me to see how relationships work in this world. It's as if books give me an inner glimpse into what I'm eager to learn about as well as prepare me for new experiences that are headed my way.

I was a bold little girl, as curious and independent as Pippi Longstocking. Reading stories about this fictional girl kept me from feeling as if there was something wrong with me, especially times when I felt my own inner strength. That could be why Pippi Longstocking books are my all-time favorite children's books.

While reading Judy Blume books, I learned that I wasn't the only kid who wondered what God really was. I also learned that I wasn't the only child who wondered if God even heard my prayers. Other things that I learned was that no one in this world was seemingly *perfect*. There was this sense of kinship and connectedness that I gained from reading these and other good books.

Later, as an adult, ideas of what I could do as I continued to evolve in this world blossomed more. Reading autobiographies and biographies of people who had overcome hard childhoods to fulfill their dreams and enrich the world empowered me to know that I, too, could overcome childhood challenges and do great things.

There are also physical benefits gained from reading good books. Among those benefits, there's:

- Brain stimulation
- Enhanced memory
- Stress reduction
- Improved development of the brain's occipital lobe
- Broader vocabulary
- Increased emotional intelligence
- Stimulated imagination
- Better visualization

It's amazing just how much can be gained from reading good books. No wonder books are among the most often used tools employed to teach. Add in brain benefits associated with reading and rewards derived from books grows.

Fortunately, today there's a larger variety of books available to read. For instance, there are a lot more African American children's books, middle school books and adult fiction than there was when I was growing up. Another win is that characters in novels have a lot more diverse backgrounds.

Even more, if you convince yourself that you don't have time to read good books, there's the option to listen to audiobooks. The only downside is that you may not gain all of the brain benefits that you'd get if you sat down and read a book. But, the stories that you'd read would still be entertaining and engaging.

"Whenever you read a good book, somewhere in the world a door opens to allow in more light."

Vera Nazarian

List Your Favorite Books – Then, Add in 10 New Books You'd Love to Read

_____

_____

_____

_____

_____

_____

_____

_____

_____

_____

Week 9
Face Your Fears

Fears seem powerful because they are fueled with intense emotion. In fact, it may be the intense emotion that false beliefs (fears) generate that you dread most. That single emotional experience could find you living as if you're looking over your shoulder, expecting some unfortunate experience to track you down and hurt you.

For sure, it can feel overwhelming. Here's the catch though. Your own thoughts, your own mind is creating the fear that you're experiencing. Little did I accept this years ago when I was wrestling fear that had built into anxiety. The battle with fear was so ongoing, seemingly harming me day and night, that I kept seeking solutions.

Finally, I came across a book about a Buddhist practice. I tried this one exercise that, as a Christian, I was initially reluctant to try.

The exercise was to sit and become aware of my thoughts. I sat on my bedside and watched my thoughts as if I was watching clouds float by. While I watched my thoughts, I said things like, "I seem to be thinking about paying my rent." Or "I seem to be thinking about a major project at work." On and on I went for two to three minutes.

As simple as this exercise may sound, it worked. Before long, I realized that they were indeed *my thoughts*. This awareness helped me to calm my brain. And, this is important because fear does produce changes in the brain.

According to *Smithsonian Magazine*, "Fear reaction starts in the brain and spreads through the body to make adjustments for the best defense, or flight reaction. The fear response starts in a region of the brain called the amygdala." The magazine goes on to share that, "A threat stimulus, such as the sight of a predator, triggers a fear response in the amygdala, which activates areas involved in preparation for motor functions involved in fight or flight. It also triggers release of stress hormones and sympathetic nervous system."[1]

Left undeterred, fear can cause blood pressure to rise and cause you to develop body responses like twitches. Fear could also cause you to seek cover or an escape from the very fear that your own thoughts are causing. Cover could come in the form of bad habits such as turning to work, food or other substances to numb emotions associated with fear.

To break the cycle, practice awareness. Actually sit still and observe your thoughts. You could do this during meditation or while simply sitting still. Another way to become aware of your thoughts and how you could be scaring yourself is to write about experiences in your life that find you feeling fear, depression, anxiety, anger (a form of fear) or hopeless. I have found that simply writing down what I'm worried about or afraid of reduces the fear.

Getting outside in nature, talking with friends, prayer and listening to uplifting music and reading empowering books are other ways that you could reduce fear. If this doesn't work, consider seeking support from a licensed, experienced and ethical therapist. If you do partner with a therapist, make sure that you have a safe, trusting relationship with the therapist.

Here are more actions that you could take to reduce and eliminate fear:

- Practice awareness and get clear about what is causing you to feel the emotion "fear"
- Forgive yourself and others for holding you to the past
- Breathe fully for two to three minutes when you feel the emotion of fear
- Shift your body (i.e. turn in a chair, look up at the ceiling instead of the floor)
- Explore a new, safe environment
- Get outdoors in nature

- Identify clear actions that you can take to address and move away from what is causing you to feel fear. Yet, do not repress or run.
- Pray, seek the Creator's guidance and trust that you'll receive that guidance.
- Take wise action.

Letting go of fear takes mind discipline. Be honest and practice observing your conscious thoughts. Pay attention to what you're focusing on throughout the day and night. And, feed your mind positive, love-based thoughts. For me, this meant no longer watching the news starting when I was nine years old.

You may also find it helpful to remember that change, a cause of fear for many, is constant in this world. While you remind yourself of this, also tell yourself that you have it within you the resources, knowledge and ability to get through anything that you could face.

"Men are not afraid of things, but of how they view them."
Epictetus

Resources:

1. https://www.smithsonianmag.com/science-nature/what-happens-brain-feel-fear-180966992/

List 3 to 5 Fears That You Are Going to Face and Remove This Year

_____

_____

_____

_____

_____

_____

_____

_____

_____

Week 10
Reach Out to Key Contacts

It's no secret that growing up in a loving family offers lifelong rewards. Growing up surrounded by mentally and emotionally healthy people gives your life structure. You can feel worthy of love and goodness and safe. Yet, as much love as you might receive while growing up, there will never be a time when you won't need love.

Keeping in touch with friends is a way to keep giving and receiving love. Mayo Clinic shares that, "Friendships can have a major impact on your health and well-being."

In addition to gifting you with opportunities to give and receive *real* love, maintaining healthy relationships offers a host of benefits. Among those benefits are:

- Strengthens your sense that you belong and, again, are loved
- Reduces stress and anxiety
- Enhances your self-esteem or your perceptions of yourself
- Provides support should you experience trauma or challenges
- Gives you the strength of connectivity

- Helps you to understand others and how you are not alone should you struggle to fully understand and navigate your way through the world
- Improves communication
- Offers hope and helps you to build more healthy relationships that are built on integrity, love, honesty and trust

Mayo Clinic shares that, "Friends also play a significant role in promoting your overall health. Adults with strong social support have a reduced risk of many significant health problems, including depression, high blood pressure and an unhealthy body mass index (BMI). Studies have even found that older adults with a rich social life are likely to live longer than their peers with fewer connections."[1]

Yet, it doesn't always seem easy to make and maintain good friendships. As with anything, a first start to developing and maintaining healthy relationships is to be a friend. As a pastor at a church I used to attend once said, "to have a friend, be a friend."

Developing and maintaining healthy relationships requires focus and commitment. So, commit to taking smart actions that lead to good relationships. Also, be wise. Not everyone who appears friendly is currently inwardly healthy enough to enter your life with integrity, care and love.

Here are some steps that you could take to develop and nurture healthy relationships:

- Attend events in your passion field. For example, if you love cars, you could attend NHRA races and auto shows.
- Introduce yourself to attendees, being careful not to share too much personal information.
- Join engaging conversations at these events.
- Reconnect with former high school and college friends.
- Accept invitations to attend events in public places. Let two to three people know where you're going and who with until you get to know new contacts.
- Join book clubs, worship center discussion groups and volunteer associations that align with your personal interests.
- Listen to and trust your inner guidance.
- Telephone and visit long-term friends and family at least once a day or once a week. Ensure that you are reaching out and letting others give you love regularly.
- Send cards and notes to friends and family.
- Go to holiday events and local festivals with friends and family.

- Be there for your friends and family.

- Show people that you genuinely care.
- Make time for loved ones.

Life may be mostly about relationships. You'll certainly always be in a relationship, even if it's only with yourself. Taking the time to nurture good relationships can strengthen your health. It can cause you to experience well-being. In fact, you might feel more passionate, positive and hopeful as your relationships deepen, expand and improve.

"Friendship is a living thing that lasts only as it is nourished with kindness, sympathy, and understanding."

Mary Lou Retton

Resources:

1. https://www.mayoclinic.org/healthy-lifestyle/adult-health/in-depth/friendships/art-20044860

What 3 Friends Are You Going to Connect with in a Love-Based Way Today?

_____

_____

_____

_____

_____

_____

_____

_____

_____

Week 11
Get Out There!

Take chances! Do something new each week!

It's easy to slip into routines. Depending on the action, it could take anywhere from 15 minutes to 66 days to develop a habit, as shared in *Psychology Today*.[1] The shorter amount of time that it could take to develop a routine might feel inviting, especially if you're trying to establish a new, welcomed routine.

Let's say you're trying to create a routine where you walk for an hour before you start work. Get your brain to create that routine within just 15 minutes of morning walking and you might feel exuberant. Even more, you might feel as if something *magical* happened.

On the other hand, should you desire to stop drinking soda and, instead, swap the sugary drink out for three glasses of fresh water, it might frustrate you to discover that two months have passed and you're still drinking soda. Yet, here's the thing.

If you don't get out there and take new actions, you'll never make the switch from soda to fresh water. You'll never add a relaxing walk to your day.

In fact, you'll be on the path to creating a life where each new day looks oh-so-much like the day before.

Keep this up and don't be surprised if you start to feel bored and frustrated, not to mention disillusioned, depressed and stuck. After all, could keeping yourself from change be a way to keep yourself bound to the past?

Why would you want to do that?

Other reasons to get out there and try something new include:

1. Embarking on new experiences is an effective way to build confidence in yourself. This is important because, although you might believe in a Higher Power or another person, if you don't believe that _you_ can do something, you may never try to achieve that thing. You might never get to the change that you really want.
2. Opportunities that you are not aware of could escape you if you don't launch out.
3. New adventures provide excellent learning opportunities. What you learn while trying new things could be used in other experiences, taking you higher and higher.
4. Excitement about each day may arise. Venturing into newness brings an air of unexpectedness. You definitely won't be able to predict what's

coming next, and why would you want to do that . . . all the time?

5. Each new tasks that you take on could introduce you to fascinating people you might otherwise never meet.
6. Taking on smart risks broadens your communication skills, vocabulary and understanding of others.
7. Continual learning is a sure advantage associated with getting out there and trying new things.

Routines that never change might lend the feeling of safety. Howbeit, stick to routines too long and you could start to feel bored and stagnant. You might also find yourself slipping into depression.

Most of all, living in the rut of unchanged routine could keep you from amazing experiences. You might never meet your best friends, soul mate or business partner if you keep doing what you've always done. You also might never reach the success that you've been longing for. So, get out there and try something new!

"Boredom could be a clue that it's time to get out there! Shake things up in smart, loving ways!"
Author Denise Turney

Resources:
1. Stop Expecting to Change Your Habit in 21 Days | Psychology Today

What New Experiences Are You Going to Open Up To?

_____

_____

_____

_____

_____

_____

_____

_____

_____

_____

Week 12

Strengthen Friendships – Who's In Your Circle

Be blessed with just one genuinely good friend and your life might start to fill up with a sense of belonging. In fact, that's a major advantage of journeying through this world with a friend. You'll feel like you belong. Better yet, you'll feel wanted, loved, valued and treasured.

The reach of friendship is far and deep. Friendships can lead to lower stress levels, better emotional intelligence and improved communication skills. Because of friends, you can also navigate your way through worldly challenges, maintain a healthy sense of hope and tap into inspiration.

Studies have also shown that the more genuine social connections you have, the better your overall health might be. Live About shares that, "A recent Harvard study concluded that having solid friendships in our life even helps promote brain health."[1]

According to Harvard Health, scientists have found that social connection "helps relieve harmful levels of stress, which can adversely affect coronary arteries, gut function, insulin regulation, and the immune system."[2] On the flip side, scientists discovered that lack of good social connections may contribute to depression.

To bring it home, consider this. "One study, which examined data from more than 309,000 people, found that lack of strong relationships increased the risk of premature death from all causes by 50% — an effect on mortality risk roughly comparable to smoking up to 15 cigarettes a day, and greater than obesity and physical inactivity."[2]

Benefits aside, genuine friendships don't just happen. As with any good relationship, to develop, deepen and thrive, friendships require work. They require thoughtfulness and tending to.

You definitely need to clearly express your appreciation for your friends . . . to your friends. Let your friends know how much you love and appreciate them. Leave no doubt in their minds about how happy you are that they are in your life.

Find ways to do this regularly. Several actions that you could take to demonstrate your appreciation for your friends include gifting your friends with flowers, calling your friends simply to say "Hello! Thank you for being such a good friend" and treating your friends to lunch.

And who doesn't love a relaxing walk through nature, an evening dancing, taking in a live stage play or a live musical performance? Better yet, ask your friends what they want to do on a weekday evening or over the weekend.

While you do this, consider the fact that some of your best friends might also be relatives. I can tell you, hands down, that my best friend is my sister. Connecting with her is on my priority list. Over the years, I've learned that good relationships take work. I've also learned that good friendships are worth cultivating and nurturing.

"Wishing to be friends is quick work, but friendship is a slow ripening fruit."
Aristotle

Resources:
1. Why Friendship Is Important (liveabout.com)
2. The Health Benefits of Strong Relationships - Harvard Health

How Are You Going to Show Your Friends How Much You Appreciate Them?

_____

_____

_____

_____

_____

_____

_____

_____

_____

Week 13
Trust The Process

Trust the process for the unfolding of your life journey. Also, trust the process of specific goals that you want to achieve. Admittedly, this is, at times, easier said than done. The force of desire can be hard to ignore. When you want to experience an event or emotion, you don't want to wait for that experience to become yours.

Still, there's advantage in waiting. It may be helpful to consider that you're waiting for parts of yourself to accept a change. You also might be waiting for your preconscious mind to process a new idea, belief, etc. before it shows up in your conscious awareness.

Another factor that could delay you receiving what you want has to do with your beliefs. Conflicting beliefs connected to a desire could cause delay. So too could your beliefs associated with what you think you *deserve*.

For instance, if you told half a dozen lies during your adolescence and then stole a video game from a store as a teenager, you might have convinced yourself that you deserve to be punished. You also might have convinced yourself that you are not worth experiences that are good.

Signs that you're doing this include constantly backing away from applying for senior level jobs or projects and continuously making money decisions that hold you back from living in a more reliable apartment or house. In these examples, you could work three jobs and still never have enough money to experience the type of lifestyle that you keep swearing you want.

This is where speaking positive affirmations and using positive visualizations could have impact. Depending on how ingrained your beliefs are, it could take months or years for you to see results. However, if you really want what you say you want, you'll keep at it.

There's another reason to trust the process. You may not be aware of the full plan for your life or how your life connects to everything in creation. In other words, trust that your life is part of a Divine plan. Stay focused on the good that you want. Take inspired action and have faith that you are being guided.

Also, ask questions. Actually ask the Creator for guidance, comfort and assurances. Tell the Creator how you're feeling and thinking, again asking for help. It also helps to practice awareness and to be honest.

You'll especially appreciate this if your desire takes years to manifest.

When you practice awareness, you pay attention to conscious, preconscious and subconscious messages that you feel. These messages may come in the form of symbols, thoughts, ideas or emotions. For example, if you want a loving, monogamous relationship and feel irritated when you imagine yourself in such a relationship, you might be dealing with unconscious conflict.

A part of your mind might not believe that you deserve a loving, monogamous relationship. Becoming aware of this emotional conflict could help you to identify a specific belief that you need to work on, eliminating and replacing the belief with a true versus a false belief.

Furthermore, in this instance, practicing awareness and honesty could help you to know which specific prayers to ask, which positive affirmations to speak and where to focus your positive visualizations. As you continue to practice awareness and pay attention to guidance that comes through dreams, emotions, symbols, etc. and as you continue to have faith and trust, you may experience the wonder of amazingly good doors opening for you.

Note: Other books that could assist you as you trust the process are the Bible, <u>A Course In Miracles</u>, <u>The Law of Attraction</u> and <u>Awaken The Giant Within</u>. I am rooting for you! You're going to win! I know it!

"Trust the process. Your time is coming. Just do the work and the results will handle themselves."
Tony Gaskins

What Are You Going to Stop Trying to Force?

_____

_____

_____

_____

_____

_____

_____

_____

_____

_____

Week 14
Capitalize on Opportunities

When I was a kid, I thought that it wouldn't matter if I let opportunities pass me by. Back then, I was certain that open doors would appear seemingly at will. If I let an opportunity pass, I told myself that I'd get another chance (and soon – at that).

It seemed to be the case. Then, I said a prayer, saw an opportunity and let that chance to get what I wanted pass. I watched the opportunity pass as if I was merely watching a boat go down a river.

Days later, when I looked for another related opportunity and none appeared, I felt fear. Further into the year, when the opportunity didn't swing back around again, I felt a mix of fear and anger.

That happened several times before I realized that just because an opportunity shows up once doesn't mean that it will appear again. It's for this reason that I lovingly encourage you to capitalize on opportunities.

Opportunities that you're presented with could be part of your life process, the very process that you're advantaged to trust. Should you experience fear, doubt or confusion when opportunities show up, be still. Notice is there's a belief or even another emotion hidden beneath the fear.

If the opportunity looks "too big", see if you can break it down into small pieces. For example, if you're offered the opportunity to serve as president on a non-profit board, ask if you can co-president the board. That, or you could ask if you can serve on the board in another capacity. As you become familiar with serving on the board, including becoming familiar with what each board role is responsible for, you might become increasingly confident in your ability to serve as president of the board by yourself.

The aim is to not let good opportunities go. Instead, capitalize on the right opportunities. To get from where you are right now to where you want to be, you're going to have to take smart risks and capitalize on the right opportunities. You'll have to face fears, make the right decisions and take wise action.

Sitting and looking at an opportunity with wonder is just not enough. Doesn't matter if it's a relationship, work, project, educational, artistic, financial or other type of opportunity. To benefit from opportunities, you have to take the right actions.

*"Teachers Open The Doors, But You Must Enter
By Yourself."
Chinese Proverb*

List 2 to 3 Opportunities You're Going to Accept This Month

_____

_____

_____

_____

_____

_____

_____

_____

_____

_____

Week 15
Travel – Explore New Environments

Traveling to new places leads to learning, understanding and intrigue. Visit a new town or country and you will have no choice but to admit that there's a lot about this *new place* that you simply do not already know. To make your way in this new environment, you'll have to ask questions, get out and meet people and try new things.

No wonder traveling to new environments can help you to shift. Gone is the ego illusion that you (or it) knows everything. Depending on the reason that you're traveling, in addition to the aforementioned benefits, you could return from your travels inspired, motivated and with answers to questions that had previously alluded you.

Fortunately, you don't have to invest in airline, train or other travel tickets to explore new environments. Short local day-trips that don't cost more than a bike or car ride can lead to unknown learnings.

When you travel, you also gift yourself with the chance to learn a new language, share your story with people living in other places and see the thread of love that connects all creation. Travel and you get to see that firsthand, not as someone listening to another traveler tell you all that she has gained from visiting new places.

Each time you travel to a new environment, you might become more creative. Should you be a dancer, painter or writer, you might find yourself visited by new visual and story ideas. Connections that you have with your family, friends, neighbors and colleagues might deepen.

What once bored you may take on an interesting aspect. Life may become a bit of a mystery to you again, causing you to feel more engaged and a part of the overall process of living.

Try it. Start small. Enter your attic, basement or another part of your home that you haven't been in for months. See if you don't feel different. Notice if you aren't more curious. Who knows? You might even have dreams that are connected to this place, dreams that could hold clues to what you should do next in your physical journey.

Another action that you could take is to drive into a residential neighborhood that you have yet to explore. If you like to fish, try fishing in a different river or lake. Bike rider? Ride your bike through a different area. Practice awareness and safety. See if you don't feel differently.

More reasons to travel into new environments are to restore or strengthen emotional and mental stability and to offer more clarity to your thoughts. Get out and travel to new places and you could also:

- Put your everyday issues in a balanced state - As you get out and meet new people, you'll see that everyone meets challenges. You'll see that the chance at success, peace, love and joy is also available to all.
- Self-consciousness may diminish, especially as you notice how others display a lack of confidence that exhibits as concern about what another person is thinking about them.
- Altered perception – Travel is a great way to shift perception. You may discover that things you thought were true simply aren't. And, what a blessing these discoveries are.
- Confidence to exit comfort zones - It takes courage to travel. The more you travel, the stronger your confidence may become.
- Habit changes – In addition to acquiring new dining habits, you also might start new exercise routines.
- Sharpened awareness – Your inner awareness might sharpen as you venture into new territory.

Forms of travel like airplanes and automobiles have made the world appear smaller. Gone are the days when it took half an hour to get across town. Now, you can be in a different neighborhood in less than 15 minutes. As small as the town that you live in (or the world, as a whole) may appear, there's so much more to discover.

Set sail! Take flight! Hit the road in a camper or RV! Explore a new hiking trail! Again, all while practicing awareness and being safe. Have fun! Get creative! Happy travels!

"The world is a book and those who do not travel read only one page."
St. Augustine

List 4 or More New Places You're Going to Visit This Year

_____

_____

_____

_____

_____

_____

_____

_____

_____

_____

Week 16
Stay Flexible

Flexibility is defined as being adaptable, a willingness to bend and change. There may be few good examples that display the value of being flexible the way that trees do. Large, old trees like the sarv-e-abarkuh, redwood, oak, elm and llangernyw yew trees endure fierce storms. Furthermore, some trees are wind resistant, allowing them to make it through harsh weather conditions.

To be wind resistant, trees require ample root space. Trees that are planted in rows, again with enough space between them, can also stand strong even when winds are fierce. Smaller trees like the palm tree withstand storms by bending with versus against the wind.

Yet, having good, deep roots and yielding or adapting to change doesn't just benefit trees. You also benefit from a rewarding childhood that provides you with good roots (also referred to as anchors). Willingness to adapt and be flexible is also important.

This isn't simply because storms may rise as you journey through this world. It's also due to the fact that change is certain. Try as you may, you can't stop change. Sure. You can try, even recruiting other people who are afraid of the changes that scare you, to help you ward off change.

But, you won't succeed at this over the long-term. Instead, you might be left feeling unheard, disappointed, frustrated, angry and maybe even depressed. If you're feeling antsy about an approaching change or a change that has recently occurred, consider practicing awareness.

Pay attention to what you're thinking and feeling. Howbeit, don't just paying attention. Be honest with yourself about what you're thinking, feeling, believing and anticipating. Imagine that the change will usher more success, happiness, balance and peace into your awareness.

Open up to the idea that the fear-based images and thoughts you might be having could be in error or wrong. This is an ongoing practice as, again, change is always happening. The thing is that you only notice so much of the countless amounts of change that are happening around you, even right now.

That means, in some form – even if you are unaware of it – you are adapting. In some ways, you are being flexible.

To improve your flexibility, release attachments. Nothing or no one in this world is truly yours. People transition, pets pass away, jobs change, houses deteriorate and more. Therefore, let go of attachments.

Another thing that you can do is to accept when you make a mistake. Avoid beating yourself up if you make a mistake. Instead, learn from the experience. Use lessons that you learn to become stronger and sharper.

Starting in the morning, focus on what causes you to feel joy and peace. To do this, I raise my hands in appreciation to the Creator when I wake. I also get still and let the desire to connect with the Creator lead me.

Close out the evening by expressing appreciation for what you experienced during the day. Set your aim, determine which goals you're going to pursue and take action. Use analytics to determine how your actions are performing. Be open to change.

Gain the most out of being flexible by being flexible and adaptable in every area of your life. This means that you're flexible in your relationships, work, fitness pursuits, etc. Watch how being flexible pays off for you.

"We cannot direct the wind, but we can adjust the sails."
Dolly Parton

What Are You Going to Look at Differently?

_____

_____

_____

_____

_____

_____

_____

_____

_____

_____

Week 17
About Loving Yourself

As you love yourself, you change every area of your life. When you love yourself, you also start to erase and replace programming mistakes that your parents or caretakers made while they were raising you. In the event that you've gotten into the habit of beating yourself up, start with small steps.

Ways that you could do this include standing in front of a mirror in the morning and saying, "I love you" to yourself three times. Do this again at night before you retire to bed. The key is to start making decisions and taking actions that *prove you love yourself*.

Definitely be patient with yourself. And forgive yourself when you make mistakes. After all, making mistakes is part of growth. It's a part of learning. Other than accepting that making mistakes is a part of learning, consider this.

Each time that you forgive yourself, you free yourself up to try new initiatives, practices and ways of thinking. Another way to prove that you love yourself is to treat yourself to three things that you love each day.

Mine includes listening to jazz or another smooth music form that I love. Soaking in a hot bubble bath and walking in nature are other actions that I treat myself to. What's your list look like?

While you think of ways to prove that you love yourself, ponder what love is. Actually think about what love is to you. For example, is love infinitely patient to you? This ties back into forgiveness.

Is love strong displays of affection to you? Or love might be honesty, openness, sincere communication, warmth, embrace, friendliness, giving and receiving, excitement, fun and laughter. Because love endures all, you may feel loved when you're there for yourself. You don't give up on yourself even if you feel embarrassed, alone or as if you keep slipping up.

Also, what do you do for friends when you want to let them know that you love them?

Why not do these things for yourself?

"Love is the Source from which we spring, create and have our being."
Author Denise Turney

Share Three Ways You're Going to Prove That You Love Yourself Each Day

_____

_____

_____

_____

_____

_____

_____

_____

_____

_____

_____

_____

_____

_____

_____

_____

_____

_____

_____

_____

Week 18
Practicing Faith

"Now faith is the substance of things hoped for, the evidence of things not seen." This Hebrews chapter 11 and verse 1 quote from the Bible is one of my favorites. Faith fuels manifestation.

A hidden element of faith is that it works with desire. That's revealed here, "things hoped for". One of the tough parts about faith for me is the "evidence of things not seen" part.

Early in my novel writing career, I absolutely believed that I would sell thousands of copies of my books within a year. Then, I published my first book, Portia, and started to get the word out about Portia, a classic inspirational novel written in memoir format.

In no time flat, I started to learn how much work goes into book marketing. Here's a few things that I did in effort to marry desire, hope and faith. I created, copied and posted flyers around cities near my residence, including in the city that I lived in. Additionally, I reached out to radio stations and scheduled and conducted radio interviews.

Other actions that I took included public speaking, attending book and cultural festivals, book signings, creating my author website, creating The Book Lover's Haven and starting my own Off The Shelf Books Talk podcast. Sending direct mail, designing t-shirts that had my book covers on them and partnering with my father to create car magnets advertising my books were other steps that I took.

Sharing this because I want to show that, despite the many targeted actions that I took, what I had hoped for didn't show up. Faith may require persistent and consistent effort. The good news is that, if you really want something, you'll do what it takes to get it.

Here's a tip. You could protect yourself from falling into the temptation to quit should faith not produce immediate results if you test faith out. Start with something that you really want and that you think is easy to obtain.

Ask to receive this experience through prayer. Follow higher guidance or sound inner promptings. Stay open and watch what happens.

Keep doing this to strengthen your faith. You're definitely going to need to be open to change and stay adaptable and flexible. What you don't want to do is to give up or stop believing in the good that you want.

"Faith is the fuel that helps to create a joyous life."
Author Denise Turney

Spotlight How You've Practiced Faith This Month

_____

_____

_____

_____

_____

_____

_____

_____

_____

_____

_____

_____

_____

_____

_____

_____

_____

_____

_____

_____

_____

Week 19
Use Spiritual Vision

It has been said that the body's eyes are not capable of seeing what can guide you toward goodness. That presents a tightrope situation, at best. Here you are in a world where you depend on physical eyesight or other senses. Yet, inner guidance does not rely on physical senses.

Fortunately, there's help. You can tap into your spiritual vision. Prayer is effective at sharpening your spiritual vision. In addition to asking for an experience that you want, pray for your spiritual vision to be opened.

Perceiving yourself in a way that lines up with how the Creator knows you can also help to open and sharpen your spiritual vision. Remember that you are not what you do, say or believe. You did not create yourself. You are what God created you as. That's worth remembering. Simply reminding yourself of that could help to keep you balanced and in a state of trust.

As it regards trust, bless yourself and trust promptings that are rooted in love. Take action when you receive spiritual guidance. You could also ask someone who is in good alignment with Source to pray with and for you.

Throughout my journey, I've also discovered that simply desiring to use spiritual vision has been a major key in awakening. Simply wanting to awaken and use right vision (also referred to as spiritual vision) has produced results.

In addition to desiring spiritual vision, I have found that following inner guidance is crucial. After all, it's not enough to want to arrive at a new location or to have a specific experience. You have to do what is required to get to where you want to be or to experience what you want.

Years ago, I would pray, exercise faith and wait for what I wanted to *magically* appear. I love trusting God. But, I clearly wasn't, as I wasn't *finishing* the achievement process. I had to use my spiritual vision *and take the right actions* based on what that vision revealed and what God wanted me to do.

Simply put, using spiritual vision is not about feeling special or important. Spiritual vision is about knowing what to do now. The vision may come through dreams, symbols, conversations or an inner feeling that you know, absolutely know, is love-based guidance.

When you receive inner knowing, pray for guidance. Follow the guidance even if what you're directed to do isn't yet reflected in the world. Also, pay attention to visions that you receive (they're like seeing a movie scene in your mind). I've experienced at least two of these types of visions. Both times, what I saw in my mind came to pass. Despite the fact that years passed before the events showed up in the world. Yet, show up they did.

Recalling those two instances just brought this to mind. Rather than assuming that you know what the vision means, pray and ask for guidance to understand what your spiritual vision is showing you. It may help to think of inner visions similar to guidance dreams.

At first glance, you might not know what the visions mean. So, ask what they mean and what actions you should take.

"True vision is within."
Author Denise Turney

In Which Ways Was Your Inner Vision at Work This Week?

_____

_____

_____

_____

_____

_____

_____

_____

_____

_____

Week 20
Stay Free of Magical Thinking

Imagine that every wish that you have, I'm talking about things that you really want to come true, would come to you simply because you wished for them. To spice it up, maybe you get whatever you really want simply by closing your eyes and saying, "Let it be so."

Talk about easy. Journeying through this world would be a cinch. If that seems appealing to you, this belief could be at work behind the scenes in your thought world. Instead of taking the right actions to get what you want, you might be speaking what you deem to be "special words" or "special phrases" and then waiting for those "special words" or "special phrases" to go out and get you what you want.

Admittedly, this may not be comforting. However, you could be engaging in magical thinking. Check this out. Britannica defines *magical thinking* as, "the belief that one's ideas, thoughts, actions, words, or use of symbols can influence the course of events in the material world." Furthermore, "magical thinking presumes a causal link between one's inner, personal experience and the external physical world."[1]

Here's what Study shares about *magical thinking*. Study describes magical thinking as "the belief that an event will occur as a result of another without any cause and effect relationship. More specifically, magical thinking refers to the notion that a person's thoughts or actions, including spoken word and the use of symbols, can alter the course of events in the physical realm without a causal link."[2]

It took me years to realize *and* accept that I had practiced magical thinking. When I was younger, I thought that I could lose weight simply by wanting to lose weight and praying to lose weight. Didn't think that I had to change my diet in the least. Fortunately, I loved to walk and run. Therefore, I exercised and dropped weight. That routine worked for several years. Then, my metabolism slowed. That's when I realized and accepted that I had to change my diet to lose the weight that I wanted to let go of. Good bye, magical thinking.

Another blessing came in the form of the fact that a part of my mind prefers scientific approaches to life. Without this anchor, as one example, I might still be merely praying and hoping and wishing to find my book's target audience. I might stop at wanting to sell books without continuing to conduct research about book marketing.

Even more, I might have stopped writing books. Results would have been dismal.

This I know for certain, as I actually did slip into magical thinking for about five years. Shocked me when I looked back at my book sales spreadsheets and saw that nearly five years passed without me selling a book. During those five years, I prayed, spoke positive affirmations and hoped to receive what I wanted. What I wanted never showed up. Thankfully, I shook out of that way of thinking.

I actually started writing and publishing books again. And, I researched marketing, took smart actions and saw my book sales increase by more than 5000%.

If you want to get what you say you want, take smart actions. Research the market and/or industry that you want to work in. Make smart connections. Learn what other people did to succeed in areas that you want to succeed in. Definitely track your results.

Tracking your results will offer you clarity. It will clearly show you which areas of your efforts are working best. Results trackers (items as simple as a spreadsheet) can help you identify where to lower, maintain and increase investments.

They can also help you to stay focused and steer clear of magical thinking.

"You are far too smart to be the only thing standing in your way."
Jennifer J. Freeman

Resources:
1. Magical thinking | psychology | Britannica
2. What is Magical Thinking? - Definition & Examples | Study.com

What Have You Been Waiting to Magically Happen That You've Now Decided to Take Smart Action to Receive?

_____

_____

_____

_____

_____

_____

_____

_____

_____

Week 21
Why You Need to Celebrate Successes

Celebrating your successes is a powerful motivator. When you celebrate your successes, you build your confidence, you acknowledge your contributions and you fuel your passion to continue making progress. There's more.

Very Well Mind shares that, "Taking the time to recognize your achievements allows you the chance to pinpoint exactly what worked so that you can repeat it in the future."[1] Brilliant Living HQ says that, "celebrating your success is another tool for cultivating a success mindset."[2]

Here's another way to look at it. Very Well Mind puts it like this, "Taking pride in your accomplishments by celebrating them—even the small ones—can also boost your self-confidence and motivate you to achieve more." So, set good goals. Aim high, way beyond what you think you can do right now.

Then, celebrate your forward steps.

Yet, don't stop there. Also celebrate other people's successes. Doing so can deepen connections. It can serve as a springboard for other people to believe in their innate good, their innate potential. It can encourage people to take off the lid on their possibilities and go for their dreams.

The surprising fact is that you don't have to buy yourself anything to celebrate successes. Simply sitting down and reflecting on the good that you have achieved is a celebration. It's an acknowledgment of how far you have come.

Looking for ways to celebrate successes? Consider:

- Enjoy relaxing on the porch as you think about the latest smart actions that you've taken
- Discuss successes that your friends, family and you have made over the last three to four months over lunch (pick one of your favorite restaurants)
- Head for the beach. It feels so good to walk along the beach and look back over your physical experience.
- Travel to a local spot that you've been wanting to check out for months, perhaps years.
- Visit an art gallery or a museum. Admire the work of the artists. Let the artists' work inspire you.
- Treat yourself to a deep body massage.

- Spend an afternoon listening to your favorite songs. Break out in a dance to a few of the tunes. See if you don't feel great as you dance.

Taking smart action may not be as fulfilling as taking smart action **and** celebrating or acknowledging your successes. Reflect on what you've done. Pause after each achievement and think about what you've done. Consider which parts of the process you've enjoyed the most. Think about changes you'd like to make from this point on. Keep advancing. Keep acknowledging your goodness.

"Everyone has been made for some particular work, and the desire for that work has been put in every heart."
Rumi

Resources:
1. Healthy Ways to Celebrate Success (verywellmind.com)
2. 6 reasons why you should celebrate success (brilliantlivinghq.com)

What 10 Personal Successes Are You Finally Going to Acknowledge?

_____

_____

_____

_____

_____

_____

_____

_____

_____

Week 22
When to Stop Learning

Remember when you were a kid and you loved to learn new things? You might even have felt left out if your siblings, cousins or friends knew how to do something that you were yet to learn how to do.

Back then, you knew that there was little that you knew about the world. Hence, you were open to listening and exploring. It didn't feel like someone was implying that you were wrong or ignorant about a thing if that person gave you feedback. In fact, you might have felt cared for as you listened to feedback that someone gave you about a game you were playing or how you were preparing a food dish.

The key is to keep learning, to never stop learning regardless of your age.

If you are a parent, you're familiar with the challenge of motivating a child to keep exploring, to remain open and keep learning. About that, Scholastic shares, "We (teachers) nurture a child's love of learning by expanding on his or her own inquisitive nature."[1]

Furthermore, learning "is a process, a series of experiences that lead to the great "aha!" moments of life." As an adult, you know that learning extends far beyond a classroom. Some of the more rewarding lessons are taught at home, at work and definitely in relationships.

To keep learning, continue to meet different people and explore new relationships. These can be friendships, relationships with neighbors, colleagues and relatives who you previously rarely communicated with. Other ways that you could keep learning include:

- Enroll in free online and offline courses, especially courses that are related to your career or passion field.
- Register to attend discussion forums at work or via a non-work organization you're affiliated with.
- Read books that teach about one or more specific topics.
- Ask people questions.
- Watch documentaries about subjects you know little or nothing about.
- Visit museums and libraries.
- Check out videos and podcasts that feature speakers who have deep experience in an area that interest you.
- Each day find something to be curious about.

The more you explore and learn, the deeper your understanding of yourself, others and life may go. Because continual learning requires inquisitiveness, remain open to the fact that, as much as you may have come to know so far, there's still so much more for you to learn.

"Learning is a treasure that will follow its owner everywhere."
Chinese Proverb

Resources:
1. Teaching Children to Love Learning | Scholastic

What Four New Life Lessons Did You Gain This Year?

_____

_____

_____

_____

_____

_____

_____

_____

_____

Week 23
Meditation Shortcuts

Meditation was a path out of anxiety for me. This was years ago when I was just a few months away from being laid off from a job that I had worked for more than 17 years. Not only had I worked at this company for more than 17 years, I had made huge personal sacrifices in order to meet demands of the jobs that I worked there.

Those sacrifices included leaving my middle-school aged son at home by himself while I worked long hours. Then, there was the 70-mile roundtrip daily commute in bumper-to-bumper traffic.

By itself, the company hadn't chosen to do mass layoffs. It was late summer 2008, the time when the Great Recession was starting to cause pain, the time when financial services greed was producing a lot of suffering on and off the stock market.

Fear around what the layoff would do to my finances, coupled with frustration that my books and freelance writing career had yet to produce greater results, built into stress. It took less than two months for that continual stress to build into anxiety.

Once I reached the anxiety level, my thoughts turned dark and muddled. To say that the growing situation with the spread of the Great Recession didn't help matters would be a huge understatement. To deal with the situation, I started using an online meditation wheel.

Oddly, I haven't come across that online meditation wheel since. Due to the amount of stress I was dealing with, I didn't bother telling myself that I didn't have time to meditate, to still my mind. Instead, I made use of the meditation wheel. One time while I was using the meditation wheel, words "the art of allowing" and "a course in miracles" surfaced.

Because I'm a believer in taking smart action, I searched the terms online. Discovering that The Art of Allowing and A Course In Miracles are books, I bought the books right away. I read A Course In Miracles to this day.

Had it not been for my meditating, I may have never discovered these two books nor gained the benefits that they offer. You too can tap into insights, a still mind and Higher guidance simply by meditating daily.

Despite what you might think, you don't have to sit in a certain position to meditate. Instead, simply sit still. Start small if you resist by trying to convince yourself that you don't have time to meditate.

Think I started by meditating for two minutes. Then, I worked my way up to 10 minutes. Today, you could get a meditation lamp for about $20 from stores like Walmart. Just sit still. Don't try to think any thoughts. Let your mind be quiet. See what surfaces. If nothing does surface, keep meditating.

There are many benefits to meditating, including better sleep, improved memory, more relaxation, thought clarity, reduced stress and less emotional pain. Furthermore, the University of California Davis shares that, "Meditation, often thought of as a path to self-awareness, can also be a path to better health. Practiced for centuries in Hindu, Buddhist and Taoist communities, people use meditation today to cope with stress in a busy world."[1]

"Quiet the mind, and the soul will speak."
Ma Jaya Sati Bhagavati

Resources:
1.   10 health benefits of meditation (ucdavis.edu)

What Are Some of Your Favorite Meditation Locations?

_____

_____

_____

_____

_____

_____

_____

_____

_____

_____

Week 24
Power of a Blessings Journal

Counting your blessings is better than counting sheep on those nights when you're laying in bed wishing that you'd drift into a deep, relaxing sleep. Why? As you count your blessings, you're focusing on the good in your life. Before you know it, your thoughts may set off on a domino effect.

After this happens, you may start thinking about more and more experiences, people and events that you appreciate. You might start to feel like your cup of blessings is running over.

What you also might find yourself doing as you do more than count your blessings but also write your blessings in a journal, is shifting away from thinking about what you let frustrate you. The stain on your carpet might not demand your attention the way that it once did. Or the sound of your loved one yawning, chewing or coughing might cause less upset within you.

Among the other beneficial fallouts might be the fact that you start focusing on your love-based achievements and goals more. And, if there's someone who has blessed you who you forgot about, that person could surface as you write in your blessings journal.

Also, the more frequently you write in your blessings journal, the more you might recall people who were influential in your earlier life. Consider reaching out to these people and telling them how much you appreciate them. Get specific while sharing your appreciation.

For example, you could call and thank someone for teaching you a skill, for helping you to care for your children or for being an active listener while you shared an upsetting experience that you'd had. The more specific that you get, the more the person might see just how much you appreciate them and what they did for you.

Should you write in your blessings journal every day, at the end of the year, you can look back and see just how good of a year it has been.

"Give yourself a gift of five minutes of contemplation in awe of everything you see around you. Go outside and turn your attention to the many miracles around you. This five-minute-a-day regimen of appreciation and gratitude will help you to focus your life in awe."
Wayne Dyer

List 10 Experiences and People You're Grateful For

_____

_____

_____

_____

_____

_____

_____

_____

_____

_____

Week 25
Make Room for New

In 2010, I found another apartment. It was, to me, a step up from the apartment that my son and I had lived in for more than 20 years. More natural light came into this new apartment, an experience that I truly appreciated and absolutely loved.

As I walked through this new apartment with a property manager, I felt as if I had advanced, so-to-speak. Simply put, the chance to be able to rent this apartment was an achievement of sorts in my perception. Yet, there remained a part of me that perceived the potential change with fear.

After all, I had lived at the former apartment for more than 20 years. Over that time, I'd developed patterns and routines. Looking back, I can easily see how I could have perceived the change as a threat.

Imagine that. A change, a new experience that I wanted was perceived as a threat by a part of my mind.

Months before I moved, I went out and bought new furniture. I told myself that the furniture would look beautiful in the new apartment.

Then, moving day arrived. Fortunately, several people showed up to help my son and me move into our new apartment. During the move, one thing that I discovered fairly quickly was how much dust and dirt I had regularly missed each weekend that I had cleaned the old apartment.

You see, I had prided myself on how well I cleaned my former apartment. Was I surprised to see the dust and dirt on the floor, behind the bed, sofa, large entertainment center, etc. When I looked at the carpet, I had to remind myself that new carpet had been installed less than four years ago.

Closets that I thought I had cleaned had scratches and stains on the walls. Soon I realized that furniture and clothes had hidden all that before.

That was one insight that I gained. The other insight was gained as movers tried to get my new sofa inside the living room of the new apartment. They tried to get the sofa through the door, then through the window, something that I had never seen tried before.

Imagine how I felt when the movers told me that they could not get the new sofa inside the new apartment. It took me awhile to face the fact, but face it, I did.

Because I had not known to measure the new sofa, I had not made room for the new. The new sofa and the new apartment did not fit. Final result saw me having movers place the brand new sofa by the dumpster where someone else, who had room for the new sofa, could come and get it totally free of charge.

Then, I went to a furniture store a day or so later and measured the new sofa that I settled upon. Workers at the furniture store carried that new sofa to my new apartment. It fit easily.

There was room for the new.

You might not be moving into a new home right now. Neither might you even want to consider moving. In fact, you might be tremendously happy right where you are.

However, that doesn't mean that there won't be a time when you don't want to enter a new experience, a new job, a new home, a new financial

state, a new way of being or a new relationship. Should this occur, remember to measure the changes that you want to embed into your life. Consider the cost of investing in the new.

Make room for the new experiences that you want to enjoy. For instance, make room in your mind. Make room in your home. Make room in your patterns and routines. Make room for the new that is loved-based so that the new doesn't seem to be a burden or a wrong choice.

"Open up to love and make room for new blessings."
Author Denise Turney

What Are You Doing to Make Room for New Blessings?

_____

_____

_____

_____

_____

_____

_____

_____

_____

Week 26
Be Consistent

Are thoughts akin to actions? Possibly. What there isn't question on is whether or not behavior is action. Of course, behavior is action, you might say. This you might argue, and even in spite of the fact that thought precedes behavior.

Whether action is thought or solely behavior, to yield good results, you need to be consistent. In fact, it might be in consistency that you prove to yourself how committed you are to going one way or another.

Through being consistent you might wear away or smooth down internal conflicts that could be holding you back from the experiences that you want. Also, when you are consistent, you create structure in your life. It's this structure that might make you feel safe and confident.

Most of all, if you're trying to enjoy an experience, you might need to be consistent to keep advancing until you open up to that experience. Here's an example. Let's say that you want to make a painting that covers a large canvas. Your primary aim might be to create a painting that's rich in colors, hues, tone and texture.

As you sit down and look at the blank canvas, you might feel excitement, more alive than you've felt in months. Should you have a clear image of the painting that you want to create, one or two things could happen as you start applying color, shape and definition to the canvas.

You could feel happiness and satisfaction the more the painting starts to resemble the image that you're holding in your mind of what you want the painting to look like. On the other hand, you could feel frustration, anger and disappointment should the painting start to take on a different look and feel than what you had imagined.

So, it is with life in this world. And, that is where being consistent can pay off hugely. Focus on what it is you actually want to experience. In fact, focus on what you want to experience more than *how* you will get to that experience.

Perhaps this will help. Consider that you're dancing simply because you want to move your body while music plays. To dance is your ultimate aim, not exactly how you move your head, neck, back, arms, legs and feet.

Yet, if you truly want to dance, you won't stop. You won't stop moving even if you get tripped up.

Therefore, to be consistent, ensure that you're aiming for something that you really want.

Then, create a roadmap. Outline specific actions that you will take to enjoy the experiences that you want to enjoy. Back to the painting example, you could be consistent about buying enough canvas paper, paint brushes and paint to keep working on paintings.

Another thing that you would need to be consistent about is investing sufficient time into the act of painting to make the artwork that you desire. Should you want to earn a full-time income from painting, you may need to add marketing actions to your plan.

Also, stay open to change. The world is changing, so you'll have to adjust, adapt and change. But, don't change your goal. Don't change your aim.

Instead, continue to engage in consistent behavior. Continue to sit down and actually paint. Buy painting supplies when your supplies start to run low. Constantly invest sufficient time in your art. Soon you may produce a result that surprises even you.

"The key to success is consistency."
Zak Frazer

List 4 Ways You've Been Consistent This Month

_____

_____

_____

_____

_____

_____

_____

_____

_____

_____

_____

_____

_____

_____

_____

_____

_____

_____

_____

_____

_____

_____

Week 27
Face Facts

Earlier you read about the importance of disengaging from magical thinking, if you do, in fact, engage in magical thinking. Again magical thinking is expecting something to happen simply because you want the thing to occur.

Regardless of what you want to experience (and isn't life about creating experiences that you want) – face facts as they appear. If you don't, you could set an admirable goal only to feel lost or miserable simply because you refused to face facts as they showed up.

One way to catch yourself turning away from facing facts is to become aware of when you resist taking an honest look at where you are right now. Examples of this include:

- Refusing to step on the bathroom scale for fear that you won't like what you weigh
- Rationalizing about why you don't need to look at your bank account even if you haven't checked your bank balance and your spending for more than a month

- Not glancing at your car's speedometer when an inner message arises within you alerting you to the fact that you're driving much faster than you're accustomed to (i.e. speeding around sharp curves, down steep hills)
- Creating false stories about your relationships to avoid examining what you and the people in your life are actually saying and doing to each other

Here are actions that you could take to encourage yourself to face facts. These actions are easy to implement. If you catch yourself turning away from facing facts, you might benefit from incorporating two or more of these steps into your experience:

- Set a day or time of day to check analytics such as your bank balance, retirement account, etc.
- Review business sales and expenses once a week
- File solopreneur or small business quarterly or annual taxes on time to avoid fines and penalties
- Establish a time of day when you will lift weights and do aerobic exercises (exercises that raise your heartrate) and stick to this schedule (actually lift weights and exercise as you said you would)

- Avoid marketing tools that lack clear analytics. Review these analytics once a week.
- Meditate or sit still for at least one to two minutes in the morning and one to two minutes at night
- Determine when you will telephone, text and visit family and friends then actually connect with your loved ones as you committed to doing (do what you say you will – face facts about your relationships)

Face facts and you could steer clear of deep disappointment. That's because, by facing facts, you are open to actually seeing the results of your efforts. It may also be a sign that you're taking responsibility for your life.

"You are overcome by the fact because you think you are."
Norman Vincent Peale

List 2 Things That You've Stopped Running From

_____

_____

_____

_____

_____

_____

_____

_____

_____

Week 28
Expanding the Scope

Helping others is more than supporting charitable organizations via financial support, serving meals at food kitchens, stocking food pantries and helping to build homes. For sure, these choices are incredibly valuable. What you give to others in these and similar forms of action have deep short and long-term impact.

Howbeit, unless you're having face-to-face engagement with the person you're helping, rewards from those connections may not be as deep. Think back over the times when you've helped others. Consider when you made a financial donation to a charity. How did you feel? Did you feel as if you knew the people you were helping? Were you able to receive feedback from the people you were supporting? Or did it seem as if you were mainly sending money to an organization that's committed to helping those in need?

Compare that "helping experience" to an instance when you met with someone and helped him/her face a fear, learn to read, fill out a job application, get free of a violent relationship, rebuild her home after a fire, etc. What did that experience feel like?

Did you learn anything from the person you were helping? For example, perhaps you learned a new way to communicate with someone who is neurologically different than you. Or maybe you learned a new way to strengthen your own family based on what the person you were helping shared with you about how his family gets together weekly, celebrates holidays and cares for their young and elderly relatives.

Whether you notice it or not, when you help others, you also help yourself. This world can offer you ample opportunities to help others. If you connect with someone face-to-face, you can gain more than you might imagine. You might start to see how much you're being helped through the experience.

"Life engenders life. Energy creates energy. It is by spending oneself that one becomes rich."
Sarah Bernhardt

List 3 Ways That You Helped Others (In-Person) This Month

_____

_____

_____

_____

_____

_____

_____

_____

_____

_____

_____

_____

_____

_____

_____

_____

_____

_____

_____

_____

_____

Week 29
Commit to Love

Love has been described as being infinitely patient, caring, kind, eternal and all-powerful while, at the same time, being gentle. Furthermore, love has been described as being forgiving, truthful and equitable. Nothing is out of balance in love. Additionally, love is the absence of fear. As the scripture, 1 John 4:18 shares, "There is **no fear** in love; but **perfect love** casts out fear, because fear involves punishment, and the one who fears is not perfected in love."

How would you describe love? What does love mean to you? Depending on your experiences and on what your relatives have said about *love*, you might think that love is all about romance. Absent people holding hands, kissing and being sexual with one another, you might have come to think that love isn't present.

As someone once told me, to learn about love "keep on living." The longer you remain in this world, the more you may come to see love as having nothing to do with sex and everything to do with what is unseen. When I was a kid growing up, I could literally feel my paternal grandmother's love. Her love was so often present and strong.

She didn't have to say a word. I could literally *feel* her love for me. The experience was uncanny, something that I couldn't explain. Back then, I wondered what caused it, why my grandmother loved me so much. Now that I'm an adult, I realize that love is unseen but so powerfully felt.

Another lesson that I have gained is how love is unexplainable. You certainly can't track it or hold it in your hands. However, feel truly loved by just one person and you may start to know that you are worth receiving love, that you are worth receiving goodness and blessings.

For me, because my mother passed when I was a kid, I needed my grandmother's love. I needed her care and her tenderness. She was gentle but very strong. And, she literally searched for ways to make each member of our family feel loved, cared for and important. Just thinking about the power of love that she shared makes me realize how important and how impactful love is.

It's a blessing to recall times when someone loved me unconditionally. Fortunately, my grandmother wasn't the only person who did this for me. I don't even want to consider what I would feel like and what life would be like for me had I not been the beneficiary of people who were committed to love.

Has there been a time in your life when you questioned whether you were loved, by even one person? As much as my grandmother loved me, I have had the experience of doubting if I was loved.

Should you be familiar with that experience - and - if you've had the experience of being loved, consider contrasting the two experiences. Which one is more empowering? Which one makes you feel safe to be who you really are?

Are you open to gifting other people with the blessings of the power of love? Would you be open to making a commitment to love? Hopefully, you are.

At times, it may feel hard to keep that commitment. You set expectations that depend on another person and the other person falls short and you feel disappointed. Someone cuts you off in traffic or while you're speaking. Demands that people place upon you feel more than you can handle. A physical illness saps your energy.

There are so many events that pop up to tempt you not to love. Yet, keep the commitment to love and to _only love_. The more you do this, the easier it may become for you to love at all times, in all situations. What power you will move with then.

"We can only learn to love by loving."
Iris Murdoch

Describe a Time This Week When You Demonstrated Your Commitment to Love

_____

_____

_____

_____

_____

_____

_____

_____

_____

_____

_____

_____

_____

_____

_____

_____

_____

_____

_____

_____

_____

Week 30
Accept Truth

Truth is the gateway to good change. Being stuck in a regressive situation that's only getting worse can feel debilitating. In addition to draining you emotionally, this type of stuck-ness can put a drain on your psychological and physical health. Stay in the situation for a long period, could be months or years, and you might start to convince yourself that there's no way out of the situation.

Another thing that you might do is to convince yourself that, due to nothing that you did or thought, the situation would have happened regardless. It's as if you'd resigned yourself to believe that nothing would have prevented you from landing into this horrible situation.

But, is that the truth?

Look back over your journey and see if there was even one thing that you did, said or thought that might have helped lead you to where you are now. After you see your role in the situation (after all, you are *in the situation*), forgive yourself. Beating yourself up for making a mistake is not the path to good change. So, forgive yourself. Actually, sit down, be still and forgive yourself.

- Then, reflect on *how* you have been thinking and *what* you have been thinking about over the last several days and weeks.
- Accept what you have been thinking, believing and doing. (Years ago, I heard that a belief is no more than a thought that you've been thinking so often that you have come to accept that thought as truth.)
- Steer clear of judging the way that you have been thinking, feeling and behaving.
- Decide what you want to change and *why*.
- Identify ways that you can start to realize the change that you want to experience.
- Record your progress to avoid slipping into magical thinking or into believing that you are making more or less progress than you actually are.

Accept the truth as it reflects back at you. Keep yourself free and empowered by staying away from rationalizing. Placing blame on yourself or others may be a way to avoid accepting truth and making necessary changes. Blaming yourself or others changes absolutely nothing.

So, if you really want good change, accept truth and take smart action. It may help you to accept truth if you solicit feedback from people you trust, people who you know love you and want the best for you.

Actively listen to the feedback that these people give you around what you're seeking to know the truth about.

Also, you could tap into truth by meditating and writing down your dreams. But, don't just write your dreams down. Interpret your dreams. There are dream dictionaries that you can reference to interpret your dreams. However, over time, you might notice the same symbols popping up in your dreams. Pay attention to how you feel when you see these symbols. See if the symbols are images that you saw during your childhood or an earlier part of your life.

Journaling or freestyle writing are other ways to open up so that the truth bubbles up from your subconscious into your consciousness. According to *Psychology Today*, it can also be helpful to accept that you may not agree with truth. In fact, you may try to fight truth.

That's okay. Just because you don't like truth, doesn't mean that you can change truth. What you could do is make it easier on yourself and work to acknowledge truth early. Furthermore, *Psychology Today* shares that, "Acceptance of now is a profound and powerful step. It requires immense courage, to be honest about where we are."[1]

Even better, "When we accept what is, which includes our guttural "no" to it, we give ourselves permission to join our life, to experience the present moment as it is." And, "To accept what is offers us permission to finally be authentic with ourselves, to fully be in our own company."

"There's a world of difference between truth and facts. Facts can obscure the truth."

Maya Angelou

Resources:

1. https://www.psychologytoday.com/us/blog/inviting-monkey-tea/201902/accepting-reality-feels-unacceptable

What 2 Things Have You Decided to Be Truthful About?

_____

_____

_____

_____

_____

_____

_____

_____

_____

_____

_____

Week 31
Seek Help

Just as you might need support accepting truth, you may benefit from seeking and receiving help with other growth areas. This is a time to definitely put ego and pride aside. Because if you wait and seek help too late, you could have to work harder to reverse thought patterns, cell patterns (as it relates to physical health) and brain patterns or habit.

Signs that you may need to seek help range from an irritability that lingers. An example could be feeling irritated with the sound of water rushing out of your bathroom spigot as you wash up in the morning to then feeling irritated with the sound of a loved one breathing as you enter the kitchen. Throughout the day, routine events like a car horn going off, birds chirping and people laughing could irritate you as well. Should this occur, it could be a sign that you would benefit from seeking help.

However, it's important to note that not all help is mental health related. You could benefit from seeking help to:

- Learn how to operate a new technological device
- Prepare to become a parent

- Teach your child a new skill or classroom lesson
- Develop and market a new product or service that the company you own is scheduled to launch
- Sharpen your communication and active listening skills

As it regards mental and emotional health, you might seek help to set healthy boundaries. This could impact you at work, home and during your leisure time. Setting healthy boundaries was a big item for me, because I cared what others thought of me. Eventually, I learned that I might never truly know what anyone thinks of me. What I might simply do is take facial expressions and what people say to or about me and mix in my own perceptions of myself and then assign emotions to the final outcome.

That led me to saying, "Yes" to nearly everything that was asked of me. You guessed it. That, in turn, led to feelings of overwhelm. Therefore, it's worth it to point out some reasons why you may want to seek help for your mental and emotional health, including:

- Inability to say "no" and express your real wants.
- Personality shifts that make you feel, act and/or think as if you were another person. For example, if you're generally upbeat and you start feeling as if it's too hard to get out of bed, you might need to seek help.
- You isolate yourself from family and friends. That or you might start socializing a lot, as if you're afraid to be alone.
- Poor hygiene is another sign that you might benefit from seeking help.
- Thoughts of violence, including self-harm, start to enter your mind.
- Addictive behaviors and thoughts feel as if they leave you helpless, as if you have no control over your own life.
- Sorrow, anger, fear or anxiety seem like "normal" ways of being or feeling.
- Friends tell you that they are concerned about you.

To seek help is a show of strength. Seeking help makes it clear that you care about yourself. It also demonstrates that you realize that we are all connected and that, what you may not know, someone else does. Also, as you continue to grow and move forward, you will enter new areas. It's

during these entry points that you may find yourself
needing to seek help more.

*"There is no need to suffer silently and there is no
shame in seeking help."*
Catherine Zeta-Jones

What Did You Seek Help or Guidance on This Week?

_____

_____

_____

_____

_____

_____

_____

_____

_____

_____

_____

Week 32
Set Healthy Boundaries

Being busy used to lend me the belief that I was valued, needed. The fuller my days were, the more important I felt that I was. It reached a point where I felt guilty taking a one day vacation. Looking back on that time, I laugh. It feels absurd to me now that I once felt that I was doing something wrong or leaving the organization that I worked for in a bind if I took a day away from work.

That mindset spilled over into my personal life and volunteer work. Didn't matter what someone asked me to do or how tired I was, I found a way to appease the requester. My work as a podcast host on Off The Shelf Books has shown me that other people struggle to set healthy boundaries for similar reasons. Perhaps, the struggle to set healthy boundaries is rooted in what we think of ourselves.

Other forms of unhealthy boundaries may, unfortunately, include physical, sexual, financial or emotional abuse. Submitting to an abuser generally only makes the situation worse. I have heard this repeatedly from people who have been in domestic violence situations. This serves as just one more reason why it's important to set healthy boundaries and speak up for what is right.

Regarding why it may be hard to set healthy boundaries, check this out. According to Counseling Recovery[1], you might not set healthy boundaries because:

- You're afraid of what others will think (see above)
- Attempting to avoid conflict
- Thinking that what's being asked of you is not too big a deal (that the issue is not that important)
- Afraid to be perceived as being selfish
- Not knowing how to begin to set healthy boundaries

Ways to set healthy boundaries vary. Here's a start:

- Tell a requester that you're unable to do what they've asked of you without over-explaining
- Speak up (start doing this early in relationships)
- Clearly tell a person that you do not want to be touched
- Let people know when a comment or joke is offensive
- Listen to other people's point of views without feeling as if you have to make it your own
- Discuss your schedule with people in your inner circle, letting them know that you're not

available to babysit, be at their home when the technician arrives, walk their pet, etc. whenever they want
- Visit relatives when you feel emotionally and psychologically healthy to do so
- Avoid signing up for too many volunteer projects
- Seek help, including legal help as needed, should you find yourself being abused
- Reflect on what's going on inside yourself should you feel the need to take on extra work to feel like a "Superwoman" or a "Superman"

You teach people how to treat you by the way that you treat yourself. Another way that you teach people how to treat you is by how you *allow* other people to treat you. When you set healthy boundaries, you demonstrate that you value yourself, that you believe you have worth.

"You get what you tolerate."
Henry Cloud

Resources:
1. https://www.counselingrecovery.com/blog-san-jose/why-you-dont-set-boundaries

List 4 Areas That You Have Set Healthy Boundaries For

_____

_____

_____

_____

_____

_____

_____

_____

_____

_____

Week 33
Know That You Are Loved

Isaiah 54:10 shares that, "Though the mountains be shaken and the hills be removed, yet my unfailing love for you will not be shaken nor my covenant of peace be removed," says the Lord, who has compassion on you."

Furthermore, Roman 8:38-39 says that, "For I am persuaded that neither death nor life, nor angels nor principalities nor powers, nor things present nor things to come, nor height nor depth, nor any other created thing, shall be able to separate us from the love of God which is in Christ Jesus our Lord."

Regardless of what you think, see, hear, feel, witness or experience, you are loved. You are always loved. Another truth is that you do not have to earn love. Even if you wanted to, there is nothing that you can do to earn love. The Source that created you always loves you.

Pause and let that sink it. Soak it up. Let it become what it is – a part of your essence. Consider that the Source that created you cannot be separate from you. Loving you allows that Source to love itself and to extend love. Accept that you are loved. Receive it.

Whether you notice, see, feel or acknowledge that you are always loved, you are. The impact may become apparent when you *accept* that you are loved. That may allow you to see how many ways you are loved.

And, the truth that you are always loved can reveal itself in seemingly small ways. A smile from a stranger, someone holding a door open for you so that you can enter a building as you carry heavy boxes or a reassuring word from a neighbor as you struggle through a major life change.

Nature can also show you that you are loved. Perhaps it comes through birds chirping outside your bedroom window in the morning, a rainbow following a storm or a pet that fills with happiness each time you come home.

Pay attention and you might spot more than a dozen signs that you're being loved right now. Proof can come from what appears to be the outer world. Or proof can come from within your being. So, start looking. And, remember – you are always loved.

"Love has many faces."
Author Denise Turney

When You Looked for Proof That You Are Loved, What Loving Reassurances Did You Find?

_____

_____

_____

_____

_____

_____

_____

_____

_____

_____

Week 34
When to be Patient

Patience is part of love, as recorded in I Corinthians 13:4. It's a show of faith. When you are patient, it is as if you believe that the good that you want is *definitely coming to you.* Practicing patience is also a sign that you believe in your own abilities. You also show that you believe in the good in others when you are patient with them.

Regarding the power of patience, Mindful shares that, "patience is essential to daily life—and might be key to a happy one." Mindful goes on to say that, "patient people tend to experience less depression and negative emotions, perhaps because they can cope better with upsetting or stressful situations. They also rate themselves as more mindful and feel more gratitude, more connection to mankind and to the universe, and a greater sense of abundance."[1]

Hence, practicing patience could help to set you up for a happier life. As you practice more patience, you may experience less stress commuting to and from work, waiting in grocery store lines, sitting back and waiting for technological devices like laptops and smartphones to send messages.

If anything is worth paying attention to for me, this one is it. Since as long as I can remember, patience has not been my strong suit. Driving to and from work was a huge wrestling of impatience for me. Stress was like a second layer of skin during those commutes. It wasn't until I learned to practice patience that the traffic on my way to and from work started to let up.

Looking back, not practicing patience hurried me into states of frustration, anger and, sometimes, depression. Oddly enough, my oldest dream of making it as a full-time novelist has been the thing that I have had to practice the most patience (and smart action) with.

If I hadn't continued to be patient, I would have given up on my writing years ago. And, you wouldn't be reading this book. In addition to continuing to take smart action until you receive a result that you want, practicing patience yields additional benefits, such as:

- Practicing patience improves friendships
- Likelihood of achieving your goals may increase as you take smart action and practice patience
- Being patient could reduce stress, headaches, diarrhea, etc.

- Aim to practice patience and you could engage in more mindfulness and awareness

Tips to become more patient include become more aware of what you are thinking and feeling. Also, journal rewards that you gained after you chose patience. Make it clear to yourself just how beneficial it can be to practice patience.

Try practicing patience with yourself, others and the universe. As a tip, if you've spent years being impatient, it may take months, maybe even years, before you start to practice patience naturally. As you sharpen this skill, be patient with yourself.

It may help to reflect on how you felt when someone was patient with you. Contrast this to how your felt when someone wasn't patient with you. Prefer feelings of love and choose to practice patience. You're worth every bit of peace and joy that it will bring you.

"Patience is the companion of wisdom."
St. Augustine

Resources:
1. The Benefits of Being a Patient Person - Mindful

Celebrate 3 Instances When You Exercised Patience This Week

_____

_____

_____

_____

_____

_____

_____

_____

_____

Week 35
Active Listening

Have you ever sat within less than 10 feet of someone, seemingly listening to what he was saying, while, at the same time, not recalling much of what was said? In that case, you might have been listening so that you could respond or offer your input as it related to the topic that was being discussed.

In fact, you might not have had much interest in what any other speaker, beyond yourself, said. What might have been priority to you was ensuring that everyone heard or listened to what you wanted to say.

Depending on your role, you might be accustomed to having people actually silence when you enter a room and listen to you, as if what you think or want to say is more important than what anyone else thinks or wants to say. For instance, if you serve as a chief executive officer, pastor, founder of a business or social organization or head of a business group, people may think that it is "good practice" to place more value on what you say.

This relationship communication approach might seem effective while you are at work. Venture home and you might discover that this doesn't work so well with your spouse, partner, siblings or children. Yet, there is another point.

Namely, the workforce is changing. COVID19 ushered in several workforce changes. Workers don't want to be relegated to *perceived* lower levels based on their title, role, function or anything else. This is a good shift.

Now, regardless of your role or title, it's increasingly important to actually listen. This includes listening to everyone who speaks with you that you wish to engage in conversation with. In other words, don't listen simply to gain information. Also, listen to ensure that you understand what is being said and maybe even why the speaker is sharing what she shares with you.

To improve your active listening, try the following:

- Repeat back to the speaker key points that she shares
- Look at the person who is speaking or sharing information
- Steer clear of thinking of what you will respond with

- Offer verbal and physical feedback, such as a nod, that you are listening and understanding what the person is saying
- Ask questions if there's a point that you don't understand
- Wait until the person stops sharing information or speaking before you respond

Active listening could reduce the number of times that you have a misunderstanding. It could also lower mistakes that you make. Above that, when you actively listen to someone, you send the message that you value the person.

"To say that a person feels listened to means a lot more than just their ideas get heard. It's a sign of respect. It makes people feel valued."
Deborah Tannen

Acknowledge 10 Instances When You Actively Listened to Another This Month

_____

_____

_____

_____

_____

_____

_____

_____

_____

_____

_____

_____

_____

_____

_____

_____

_____

_____

_____

_____

Week 36
Persist as Needed

It surprises me how many people who I view as being "successful" had to persist for years until they achieved what they wanted. Some "successful" people didn't manifest their dreams until after they transitioned. Hearing or reading their stories serves as tremendous inspiration.

Primary among these people are Vincent Van Gogh, Zora Neale Hurston, Harland "Colonel" Sanders, Margo Martindale, Bea Arthur, Morgan Freeman, Wally Blume and Franny Martin. These persistent visionaries worked hard only to either have their work become successful after they transitioned or they worked hard for years only to wait to realize success in their 40s or later.

There are many more people who persisted for years before they realized the success that they'd been dreaming about. Had these determined people not persisted, we would not have artwork, technology, entertainment productions, food items and deeply impactful writings.

You already know that a dream that's been deposited into you by your Higher Self is not going to stop tugging at you. Sure. There might be times when you have to work a job to generate enough income to pay your bills.

Although this job might not be your dream, you could learn marketing, communications, time management, money management and other transferrable skills while working this job. The point is to look for ways to get lessons while working this job that can benefit you as you continue to pursue your dream.

Here are more tips that could motivate you to persist:

- Visualize yourself living your dream for two to five minutes in the morning and again for two to five minutes before you go to bed at night.
- Create something that's directly related to your dream daily or weekly.
- Attend networking events and training seminars that sharpen your skill.
- Read stories about people who persisted until their dreams came true.

"And let us not be weary in well doing: for in due season we shall reap, if we faint not."
Galatians 6:9

What 1 to 3 Goals Do You Want to Persist with Until Your Dreams Manifest?

_____

_____

_____

_____

_____

_____

_____

_____

_____

Week 37
Be Honest

Little may block acceptance of the truth the way that dishonesty does. Being honest promotes deeper communication and trustworthiness. For another take on honesty, you could be the best salesperson in the world. Yet, the second that people discover that you sold them products based on dishonest claims, that could all change. Not only could you face a barrage of outrage, you might have to deal with returns. Worst of all would be a permanent loss of business.

That's just one example of how it doesn't benefit over the long term to be dishonest. Admittedly, there are situations where dishonesty might "appear" to pay off over the short term. But, when all is said and done, it's the worst choice.

People know that they can trust you when you are consistently honest. This can prove especially true when you're honest despite the fact that what you're being honest about could seemingly set you back. For instance, if you are honest about a calculation, product development, service deadline, etc. promise that, you now realize, you're unable to keep, you could turn away a few prospects.

However, when people come to see what you could have lost and combine that with the fact that you *chose to be honest*, your trustworthiness could skyrocket. The next time that you work on a project or sell a product or service, the numbers of people supporting you could increase.

Other reasons to be honest include the fact that whether you're honest or not, you are showcasing your character. This next reason may really hit home. It takes me back to a former relationship. I can still hear myself telling my partner that lying about a mistake was worse than making a mistake. You too may rather be told the truth, even if what you hear stings, than have someone lie to you.

Why?

Dishonesty displays a lack of respect. It's as if you view yourself as "smarter" than the person you're not being honest with. Another way to look at it is as if you thought that you were so much smarter than the person that you were being dishonest with that only you would know that you were lying. So, being honest shows:

- Respect – that you respect the person you're communicating with and that you also respect yourself

- Honesty also makes life easier. It keeps things simple
- When you are honest, you also express love for yourself and others

It takes courage to be honest, this includes being honest with yourself. For instance, it takes courage to be honest and admit that you don't like the way that your life is going. Or maybe you no longer gain satisfaction from your job.

Other areas where you might have to exercise courage and be honest with yourself are around intimate relationships, where you live and the status of your health.

If you're struggling to be honest, here are a few tips:

- Reflect on what you want to say, if you're communicating with another person, or considering a decision that will impact you
- Avoid comparing yourself to others
- Envision the life that you truly want to experience
- Be direct while also being kind – get to the point
- Stay free of trying to impress
- Forgive yourself

- Choose freedom over exaggeration (which could be an offshoot of an attempt to impress)
- Allow yourself to feel how free you will feel after you accept and share the truth

"Before you can lie to another, you must first lie to yourself."
Naval Ravikant

What Have You Decided to be Honest About?

_____

_____

_____

_____

_____

_____

_____

_____

_____

Week 38
Be Willing to Change

If one thing is constant and dependable in this world, it's change. To live a champion life, you need to be adaptable and flexible. You need to be willing to change.

There may be no better way to illustrate this than to look back to what was going on in the world when you were a kid. Regardless of how old you are now, if you look back 20 years, you'll see loads of change. That change is reflected in technology, medicine, education, social landscapes and more.

As hard as it might be to imagine right now, there could come a time when humans are working alongside robots on a regular basis, in offices and factories. In fact, some auto manufacturers already have robotic equipment working alongside humans. It might seem odd to think that could happen in classrooms and corporate offices, but it could.

Fight change and you find yourself out of work. Other areas where fighting change could impact you are your personal relationships. For instance, if you're a parent, you have to be willing to change the way that you approach and communicate with your children as they get older.

It's an adjustment. When your children are newborns, they simply go where you take them. As they get older, they start to share their opinions with you, letting you know that they don't want to visit a certain relative, go to school, to the grocery store, etc. By the teenage years, your children are engaging in deep, robust conversations with you, some which you might not want to be a part of.

Same applies when communicating with your elderly parents. Add in work changes, policy changes, social changes, etc. and you could, at times, feel like the world is changing at too fast a pace.

The more flexible and adaptable you are, the better. Living in the world may feel a lot less stressful. You also might be willing to actively listen to others, truly hearing what they trust you enough to share with you.

Surprisingly, another time when you need to be willing to change is when you make progress. As you move forward with learning, growing and developing, you'll experience change. In fact, you might feel most uncomfortable as you near the edge of a massive and good change.

Exercise courage and accept that there's a lot in and beyond this world that you may not be aware of.

There's certainly a lot that you cannot control. You can't even control the tremendous success that may be waiting for you to open up and receive.

So, open up and be willing to change. Your openness and your willingness to change could be the key to you receiving what you've been praying, working and waiting for.

"Your life does not get better by chance, it gets better by change."
Jim Rohn

Open Up – What 3 Things Are You Willing to Change?

_____

_____

_____

_____

_____

_____

_____

_____

_____

Week 39
Let Go

When was the last time that you were asked to look after someone, maybe a younger sibling, or to oversee a project? In both instances, you may have felt responsible for ensuring that outcomes were successful.

Take on a project or assignment that's super easy for you and you might not even consider trying to control the project or assignment. Gone is the fear that you will fail. However, flip that scenario to a situation where you are highly doubtful that you will succeed and you might try to control more than the outcomes.

You also might try to control processes. Demand to control could create stress, anxiety and fear in you and others who you're working with the project or assignment on. To help you let go, practice mindfulness.

Practicing mindfulness offers many benefits, one being the ability to steer clear of fight or flight stressors. As *Fast Company* shares, "An excessive need to control can lead to unproductive stress, because it often puts people in an extended "fight or flight" mode."[1]

As it relates to mindfulness and letting go of trying to control outcomes, the article continues with, "Helen Weng, a clinical psychologist and neuroscientist at the University of California San Francisco, mirrors this sentiment, suggesting that we're better off focusing on the intention of our actions, rather than insisting on (or "clinging to") a certain outcome."

Benefits noted, it still might not be easy to "let go". These steps might help:

- Step away from the project and reassess your emotions
- Notice if there are unpleasant feelings that you're actually trying to control rather than a project, initiative or relationship
- Accept that change is part of the journey in this world
- Live in the now or in the present
- Exercise faith that the best outcome will be realized
- Meditate or sit still to calm and quiet your mind
- Ask for inner guidance
- Accept feedback from others who have your best interest at heart

And, learn from what you experience. Even if outcomes do not match your expectations, you could walk away richer due to the lessons and insights that you gain. Letting go also helps you to allow others to be their authentic selves. Therefore, consider approaching life with courage, faith, vision and a positive love-based expectation that things will turn out good whether you realize that in the short or in the long-term.

> *"We can't be afraid of change. You may feel very secure in the pond that you are in, but if you never venture out of it, you will never know that there is such a thing as an ocean, a sea. Holding onto something that is good for you now, may be the very reason why you don't have something better."*
> *C. JoyBell C.*

Resources:
1. https://www.fastcompany.com/90424137/5-mindfulness-techniques-for-letting-go-of-control

In Which 3 Specific Life Areas Will Letting Go Bless You Most?

_____

_____

_____

_____

_____

_____

_____

_____

_____

Week 40
Admit When You're Feeling Fear

This scripture bears repeating. "There is no fear in love, but perfect love casts out fear," from 1 John 4:18. Fear is so painful that it's an emotion that you might find various ways to try to repress or avoid. According to scripture, fear is torment. It can cause you to want to give up, flee, fight, argue, control and sit on the sidelines of your own life.

Give into fear and you could drift into a state of settling in life. Or you might merely do enough to "survive". Yet, there's hope. There's great hope.

A good way to move beyond fear is to surrender. Simply let go of outcomes. *Forbes* puts it this way, "Surrendering is a process. It won't be overnight that you think and feel differently. You have to give up all your fears, insecurities, and struggles and let in the bravery to live this life. You have to let go and say, 'Even if I don't see a way out, I will still find it. It's not over yet.'"[1]

Having a purpose or a love-based intention can also keep you moving forward, even if you feel fear. Remember that you can transform. You can change and adapt to what occurs, moving beyond fear into enlightenment.

When you look back at how much you have already faced and overcome, your ability to deal with fear could strengthen. But, first you have to admit that you are feeling fear. Otherwise, you might repress what you are actually feeling, thinking and experiencing.

This could create a blockage that you might not become aware of until it's too late. Or you could spend years reaching a success point only to start regressing. In that case, you could be stopping *at the blockage point* time and again.

Getting into the habit of practicing awareness (becoming aware of what you are thinking and feeling) could help you to avoid this. Therefore, start now to admit when you're feeling fear. Admitting that you are feeling fear doesn't make you weak.

It also doesn't mean that you don't trust God. What it does signal is that you're ready to live honestly. Even more, it signals that you're ready to move beyond what you've been afraid of and open up to new, positive experiences.

Perhaps you don't want to admit that you've been feeling fear. You may not want to admit that you're afraid to let go of an abusive relationship. In that regard, you might be feeling fear about living alone, paying your bills on your own or relocating to a different town.

A job change could be another area where you might be fighting to avoid admitting that you're feeling fear. Or perhaps it's your health, which could be a reason why you avoid getting medical exams, even if it's to have your urine and blood work done or to know what your blood sugar and blood pressure numbers are.

Being dishonest with yourself won't lead to happiness, peace or success. Today commit to admit when you feel fear. Yet, don't give in to fear. Instead, seek Higher guidance and take smart actions. Also, get into the habit of sitting still and quieting your mind.

Above all, be honest and admit what you're feeling. That way, you can pray and ask for specific actions to take to move beyond the fear.

"Each of us must confront our own fears, must come face to face with them. How we handle our fears will determine where we go with the rest of our lives. To experience adventure or to be limited by the fear of it."
--Judy Blume

Resources:
1. https://www.forbes.com/sites/womensmedia/2020/06/24/how-to-let-go-of-fear-worry-and-indecision/?sh=6afe81797834

What 2 Fears Are You Ready to Release?

_____

_____

_____

_____

_____

_____

_____

_____

_____

_____

_____

Week 41
Listen to That Still Small Voice

It's been said that our Creator does not shout. Instead, it's through a quiet mind that truth enters. A busy life can make those sayings sound like fantasy. Because when the pace of your life is fast and your days are full, with scarcely enough time to sit and rest for five full minutes, it can be hard to still your mind even enough to relax, let alone enough to hear what the still small voice is saying to you.

To hear that still small voice, you're going to have to quiet your mind. There is no other way except to make getting still a priority. It's not just going to happen. In a way, it's similar to living in the present. You have to choose to be present. You have to choose to release the past, not focus on a future that never really arrives and be fully present right now.

An easy approach is to sit up as soon as you awaken and be still for one to two minutes. You might work your way up to sitting still for 10 to 20 minutes as soon as you awaken. Do this before you wash up or shower.

Repeat this at night before you go to bed. Simply sit still. If it helps, focus on your breathing or use a meditation lamp. The point is to quiet your mind.

Should you start to think about what you're going to eat, cook or do the following day, return to focusing on your breathing or on the meditation lamp that you're using.

But, don't just listen to that still small voice. Actually do what that still small voice instructs you to do. Take love-based actions. Of course, if you ever hear guidance to do anything that would be harmful to you or another living being, don't take those actions. Instead, seek guidance and therapy, if necessary.

You could start trusting that still small voice if you also have dreams that align with the guidance that you've been receiving. The best way to hear that still small voice is to trust it. You do this by having faith and, again, taking smart, love-based actions.

Hearing that still small voice may also require an awareness that your purpose is love. If you're reluctant to trust, simply write down what the still small voice tells you. See if it aligns with scripture. Notice where it might be pointing you.

As you write down your dreams, notice if what the still small voice communicates aligns with dreams you've been receiving. See if that still small voice is an answer to a recent challenge or question that you've been facing.

Go slowly if necessary. But, at least get started. Start testing what you hear. Also, see if you don't feel loved as the communications come through. After all, the best guidance is guidance from your True, inner self.

"In quietness does the Master enter and is heard."
Author Denise Turney

What's the Last Thing the Still Small Voice Spoke to You?

_____

_____

_____

_____

_____

_____

_____

_____

_____

Week 42
Explore Your Brain

Do you think it's time that you learned how your brain works? Artificial intelligence (AI) is putting the brain and its functions center stage. Scientists and technologists are fast studying the human brain and testing how they can mirror those functions in robots and other forms of artificial intelligence.

Looking for more about artificial intelligence and the human brain connection? Here's what Tech4Fresher has to say about AI, "Artificial Intelligence is by far one of the most fascinating and astounding creations ever made in the history of mankind." They continue with, "Artificial Intelligence can be defined as a branch of computer science that can simulate human intelligence."[1]

In addition to performing simple tasks, AI can reason, make decisions and solve problems. The brain itself, generally no heavier than three pounds, is the most complex part of the human system. The National Institute of Neurological Disorders and Stroke says that, "The brain is the crown jewel of the human body."[2]

There are three major parts of the brain: the forebrain, midbrain and hindbrain. Each part controls different functions. For instance, the frontal lobe helps with reasoning and planning. This part of the brain is at work during arguments. Movement is another function of the frontal lobe.

Neurotransmitters in the brain communicate with each other. These neurotransmitters affect a range of functions, including sleep, memory, mood and muscle activity. Other things that the brain does may go nearly unnoticed yet, have a profound impact on your ability to adapt.

If you've heard the term "on autopilot" then you may be familiar with how the brain can repeat an activity to the point that you're able to do the activity seemingly without conscious input. Your brain can go on autopilot if you live a repetitive life.

Before you know it, you're craving bread or sweet beverages at certain times of the day. You also might feel sleepy at the same time of night, regardless of what has happened during the day.

At first glance, living on autopilot might feel safe. However, you miss a lot when you're on autopilot.

Consider just one time when you'd driven a mile on autopilot. It wouldn't be surprising if you'd looked up and wondered how you got where you did. Furthermore, you probably didn't recall seeing or hearing anything while you were driving while on autopilot.

The same happens in other life areas. As previously noted, you could end up eating, drinking, arguing, feeling sadness and getting drowsy at the same times and due to the same stimuli if you don't practice awareness and let your brain slip into autopilot.

Signs that you might have already done this include constant boredom, frustration and a feeling of being stuck. Fortunately, you can get your brain off autopilot. To do so, try new things.

For example, if you normally put your right shoe on first, try putting your left shoe on first. Style your hair differently. Take a bath instead of a shower and vice versa. Wash up in your guest bathroom instead of your main bathroom. Brush your teeth in the kitchen sink. Place your seasonings and vitamins in a different cabinet.

Celebrate and welcome change into your life. Give your brain the chance to sharpen. Help take your brain off autopilot.

"Learn how your brain works to gain better insight into why you do what you do."
Author Denise Turney

Resources:
1. What is Artificial Intelligence? Types of AI and Examples - Tech4Fresher
2. Brain Basics: Know Your Brain | National Institute of Neurological Disorders and Stroke (nih.gov)

In What Ways Does the Brain Function Differently Than You Previously Thought?

_____

_____

_____

_____

_____

_____

_____

_____

_____

_____

Week 43
Practice Awareness

Practice awareness and you could discover hidden beliefs and addictive patterns that are crafting your daily experiences. You could identify regressive triggers, including if there's a certain time of year or time of day when you experience an obsession or compulsion.

As a tip, it could take weeks of practicing awareness to spot a mental or behavior pattern. Once you spot the pattern, you're going to have to be honest about what you observe if you want to change the pattern.

Believe it or not, it took me several days to notice that I'd come home from working downtown and eat as if I hadn't eaten all day. I did this despite the fact that I generally eat one midday meal a day, could be a sandwich and a side.

When I worked from home all day, I didn't eat in the evening as if I hadn't eaten anything earlier in the day. Let me have felt frustration while at work and I'd almost feel compelled to come home and start eating and drinking the Kombucha beverages that I'd come to like so much.

At the same time, I wanted to lose weight. The pattern that I'd developed of eating after I came home from working outside my home would lead me away from my weight loss goal. What did I do?

Paid more attention to my behavior and made different choices. However, if I didn't practice awareness, I may not have known what I was doing. That's just one example of how practicing awareness could benefit you. It's a way to see more of what you're thinking and doing.

You have options when it comes to practicing awareness. For instance, you could get into the habit of practicing awareness if you:

- Write in a journal.
- Pause when you feel strong emotion arise within you. See if you can pinpoint when you first felt the emotion. There might be an event (i.e. something that someone said to you, the way you interpreted an expression on someone's face) that caused the emotion to surface.
- Eliminate non-necessary activities. Give yourself time to sit and rest your mind.
- Take small local, trips.
- Visit museums and other locations that remind you of your passion. For instance, if you love science, you could visit a science lab.
- Read a good, engaging novel.
- Write a letter to a relative or to a friend.
- Walk outside in nature.

- Sit on your front steps, porch or patio for an hour one day a week.
- Identify what matters most to you. Draw a graph of how your thoughts, beliefs and actions are moving you toward or away from what matters most to you.

Let go of fear about practicing awareness. You're not *making* anything happen during the practice. Instead, you're becoming aware of what is *already going on* inside your mind. In this regard, practicing awareness offers clarity and the ability to make better decisions.

"The key to growth is the introduction of higher dimensions of consciousness into our awareness."

Lao Tzu

Name 3 Things That You Noticed This Week Due to Practicing Awareness

_____

_____

_____

_____

_____

_____

_____

_____

_____

_____

Week 44
Tips to Get Creative

Self-expression can yield greater peace and confidence. The more you express yourself, the fewer parts of you feel isolated and repressed. As a byproduct, self-expression could help you to understand yourself more fully.

While you create, please set your inner critic aside. Just let your inner critic rest. You don't have to produce a work of art that lands in a museum. The point is to engage in creative arts as a way to express yourself more fully.

Here are many ways to be creative. Which of these creative ideas speaks to you?

1. Write a poem
2. Join a ceramics class and spend six months making ceramics (you could give what you make to friends and family as birthday presents and holiday gifts)
3. Plant a flower garden
4. Grow indoor plants
5. Set your breakfast, lunch or dinner plate in a creative design
6. Make your own notepads
7. Decorate your computer monitor with smiley stickers
8. Restyle your hair

9. Add a festive icing to cupcakes
10. Use family photos to decorate the outside of a photo album
11. Write a song and sing it out loud
12. Sign up for guitar lessons
13. Knit a sweater
14. Sketch a cartoon character
15. Blow up balloons and leave them in a favorite room at your home
16. Make a door wreath and hang it for the holidays
17. Write a short story
18. Make your own recipe book
19. Dance to your favorite song once a day
20. Stick colorful streamers on your bike handlebars and ride around the neighborhood
21. Send your friends and family a handmade holiday card
22. Use colored chalk to make a sidewalk drawing
23. Design a silk floral arrangement
24. Paint your mailbox if you own the property that you reside on
25. Hang colored feathers over your car's front mirror
26. Sew cool yellow cotton balls on a pair of your socks
27. Make your own mixed tape CD with you singing different types of songs
28. Decorate the top of your umbrella with your favorite cartoon figure

29. Write a positive message on your mirrors using a washable sharpie
30. Explore your neighborhood
31. Skip to your car or bike
32. Act in a local play
33. Draw a picture on a chalkboard that you hang in your den or bedroom
34. Use six different colors to decorate your fingernails with
35. Perform modern dance as part of a local dance team

Creativity brings a myriad of benefits. Included among those benefits is a sense of fulfillment, continual inner growth, more awareness, peace and inner balance. You also might sleep better at night after you engage in one or more creative arts on a weekly basis. Get creative. See what you design and create!

"One day you will wake up and there won't be any more time to do the things you've always wanted. Do it now."

Paulo Coelho

Showcase 3 Creative Arts You've Explored Over the Last 6 Months

_____

_____

_____

_____

_____

_____

_____

_____

_____

_____

Week 45
Release the Past

Holding onto the past holds you hostage to what has already happened. It holds you prisoner to what you can never change. Admit it. As hard as you may try, you have never, not once, been able to change anything that happened in the past.

What you could do if you refuse to release the past is encourage painful emotions like shame, guilt, regret, sadness and anger to resurface again and again. Also, you could start to convince yourself that what you experienced in the past is bound to repeat itself.

This single decision could keep you from exploring the world. If you had a painful relationship breakup, you might not gain the courage to date again. Or, if you do date, you might end your intimate relationships near the same time period that the first relationship ended (i.e. six months, three years).

If you stay stuck in a place in your mind, you might keep friends away. How? Should you not try new things and go new places, you could keep yourself from meeting more people. These people could be willing to share their lives with you. They could be willing to love and celebrate who you are.

Signs that you might be holding onto the past range from feeling tired even after you've slept eight hours to shifting from one emotion to another in short intervals. Although it might feel safe to stay in the past, this is a decision that has a double-edged sword. You might start to believe that there's nothing good coming your way. And, your trust in yourself and others could evaporate.

So, consider releasing the past. Take small steps if you need to. The point is to get started. One event at a time, start letting the past go. Give yourself the chance to step into a marvelous present.

Easy ways to start releasing the past are to write a letter about a painful or regretful experience that you had. Fold the letter and burn it or flush it down the toilet. Writing about an experience in a journal, including how you felt when the experience first occurred and how you feel now, may also help.

Get a deep body massage. Some people have released memories during acupuncture or a deep body massage.

Another thing that you could do is to allocate two minutes a day to experience an emotional state. At the end of the two minutes, shift your focus and start thinking about a happier experience that you've had. Don't repress. Instead, start to release the past.

Pay attention to the emotions that you're feeling. Notice where the emotions are located in your body. For instance, you might feel a heaviness in your chest or in your lower back.

Relive a scene and change the ending to an empowering conclusion. Spend time with people who mirror your value back to you.

Do something different each day. Start making room for new experiences as you release the past.

"Stop being a prisoner of your past. Become the architect of your future."

Robin Sharma

What 3 Things Did You Release This Year, Knowing That Nothing *Good* Is Lost

_____

_____

_____

_____

_____

_____

_____

_____

_____

_____

Week 46
Grieve in Healing Ways

This is a topic that I know deeply. Do I ever. Introduction to grief started when I was seven years old. At that early age, I had no idea what "death" was. On top of that, my introduction to death or transitioning came with the transitioning of my mother.

Today, I don't believe in death, so instead refer to what occurs when we exit our bodies as "transitioning". My paternal grandmother was the person who I felt safest asking where my mother was. As grandmothers often are, my paternal grandmother was empathetic.

Yet, my questions of "Where is my mommy?" "Who is Jesus" "Why did mommy leave us and go with Jesus, why Him instead of us" started to work my grandmother's patience. After awhile, she just told me that my mother was gone and to stop asking questions about it.

That's just what I did. But, I didn't stop wondering. Decades would pass before it would surface that a part of me associated big change with my mother transitioning. After that knowledge surfaced within me, I started to give myself more time to prepare for and move through a change.

For instance, instead of packing to move to a new residence over the weekend, I would give myself two months to pack little-by-little. It was a way to give myself time to adjust to the change. Even more, it was a way for me to continue to heal.

Since my mother's transition, more than 70 people I have known have transitioned. And, I'm not retirement age.

Time by itself does not heal. It's what you do with time that could help you to grieve in healing ways. Because someone close to you transitioning is a huge shift, you may associate big change with loss.

So, give yourself time to move through life changes. Be kind to yourself. Doing so could empower you to handle the unexpected.

Other healing ways to grieve include writing letters to your loved ones and listening to music that your loved one enjoyed. Releasing biodegradable balloons, lighting candles and reading autobiographies of people who were challenged with grief yet moved through grief are also helpful.

Watching autobiographical videos of people who are discussing the transitioning of a loved one and how it has impacted them may also help. Even more, this may be a good time to receive psychotherapy, even if you only go to therapy for a few months. Consider online or telephone therapy if in-person therapy is not available near you.

Also, talk about your loved one. Be prepared to receive a range of responses from people when you speak your loved one's name.

Some people may feel uncomfortable when they hear your loved one's name. It's as if they are afraid of the concept of "death" and want no reminders of what is certain to occur to them too one day.

Yet, talk about your loved one. As you do, some people might move away from you, stop visiting, texting and calling. Good friends will draw near. They might visit and simply sit with you.

Avoid isolating yourself. Reach out to others. Be the one to pick up the telephone and call family and friends. Slowly get back into the flow of life. However, don't force yourself to move too fast. Despite what you might read or hear, it could take more than two years to adjust to a loved one transitioning.

In fact, it might take more than five years, depending on how close you and the person were. Take small steps if needed. Which raises another point.

Being patient with yourself is a sure path to healing. So too is attending a support group. Worship centers and online and offline social organizations host grieving support group meetings.

There are local and mental health organizations that you can reach out to as well. As isolated as you might feel after a loved one transitions, you don't have to grieve alone.

Years later, should the opportunity present itself, be there for a friend or relative who's fresh into a grieving experience. And, continue to be loving, patient and gentle with yourself.

"It's not all about healing yourself; it's just as importantly about letting yourself heal."

Terri Guillemets

How Are You Remembering a Loved One While Staying Present?

_____

_____

_____

_____

_____

_____

_____

_____

_____

Week 47
Be Yourself

If you're not yourself, who else are you trying to be? Whoever else it is, you're going to fail at that. The only person you can ever succeed at being is YOU.

Admittedly, it takes courage to be yourself. Not everyone is going to share your opinions or beliefs. Some people might argue that the way that you think about a topic makes no sense. Others might place labels on you or tease you, saying that you are silly, too loud, too quiet, shy, outlandish, an attention seeker, etc.

If you were abused as a child, tapping into your inner courage could take work. You might have to work with a licensed therapist to get there. Adult traumas could also require the support of an experienced, licensed therapist to help you get unstuck and continue to move forward.

From deep inside a painful place, this can feel like too much. Yet, if you keep working and taking smart actions, you can move beyond the pain. Give yourself time to work through trauma and fear. Give yourself time to discover who you really are.

Don't allow people to define you. Instead, free yourself from seeking acceptance, approval and confirmation that you are good in other people's opinions and expressions when they look at you or talk about you.

And, take smart risks to exercise your confidence. Design your life in smart ways. Definitely seek ongoing guidance from the Creator. Another thing that is beneficial is to accept what you see in people.

Although we all might be love and light, that's not the place that we all operate from. You don't need to be with people who constantly criticize you, remind you of mistakes that you have made and laugh at you when you fall.

What you receive from others could reflect an unhealthy sense of self-worth to you. Therefore, surround yourself with people who you can trust. Surround yourself with people who love you, care about you and who want the best for you.

This unspoken and spoken feedback could help you to tap into the power to be yourself more. Treasure it and keep it coming into your life. Giving love to these people is also empowering. It's a way to share your true self with others.

"Being different isn't a bad thing. It means you're brave enough to be yourself."

Luna Lovegood.

Describe 10 Traits That You Love About Yourself

_____

_____

_____

_____

_____

_____

_____

_____

_____

_____

Week 48
Stay Free of Comparisons

The idea that comparing yourself to others can make you joyous or at peace is a setup. In fact, the only way that comparing yourself to others could work is if you or the person you're comparing yourself to is less than the other.

So, to begin, comparisons aren't a path to joy. Judgment is also a part of comparing. And, you never have enough information to judge accurately. Furthermore, if you don't learn to love and accept yourself, you could enter a spiral and go on to compare yourself to others for the remainder of your physical experience.

Huffington Post shares that making comparisons also damages your sense of self. But, why do we do it? "According to social comparison theory, we do this in an attempt to make accurate evaluations of ourselves," shares *Huffington Post.*[1]

Psychology Today puts it this way, "Comparing ourselves, belittling our worth, or minimizing our strengths can validate our core irrational beliefs that ultimately we are not good enough, we are unworthy, or we are not reaching our peak potential."[2]

Yet, as previously discussed, you never have all the details and information to judge or compare (another form of judgement) accurately. That alone makes comparisons a waste – a waste of time, a waste of energy, a waste of thought.

When I practice awareness and notice that I'm comparing myself or what I've done to another person or what someone else has achieved, I feel out-of-sorts. I also feel frustrated with myself. But, I work my way through this. Yet, it still amazes me that I am even tempted to compare myself to anyone else.

And, it still amazes me that I can feel unloved if someone treats another person as if they think that she's smarter or better than I see myself. That's the key. Comparison has to do with how you see yourself.

Think about it. Could you be looking for a reason to value or not value yourself? Is that why you compare yourself to anyone else? If not, why do you think that you do it?

Try this to get free of comparisons:

- Look at people when they speak with you. Make slow efforts if needed.
- Stand in front of a mirror and speak, "I love you" to yourself 10 times in a row. Do this

once a week. See if you don't start to feel different, better.

- Accept that everyone deals with fear and is trying to awaken.
- Know that just as you make mistakes, so do the people who you admire or look at as if they are giants.
- Write down your successes. Look at them and accept that *you did that good work.*
- Receive and give love and kindness.
- Distance yourself from people who choose not to be loving toward you.
- Express appreciation for beauty, light and love that you see or experience.

Keep at it, making adjustments as necessary. Also remember that a good life is ongoing work.

Remind yourself that there's no need to strive to outdo anyone. After all, no one will ever be more important than anyone else. Should you be tempted to make comparisons, remember that you didn't create yourself. At your core, you are what you were created to be. You're an extension of love.

"Comparison is the death of joy."
Mark Twain

Resources:

1. Why You Should Stop Comparing Yourself to Others | HuffPost Life
2. Why You Should Stop Comparing Yourself to Everybody Else | Psychology Today

How Does Comparing Yourself to Others Keep You from Being Who You Really Are?

_____

_____

_____

_____

_____

_____

_____

_____

_____

_____

_____

Week 49
Breathe

Someone once told me that taking in a deep breath is like ingesting the essence of life. "Breathe deeply," the person told me. "Take in deep breaths." Funny thing is that I thought I already was breathing deeply. Despite what I thought, the person told me that I generally took in shallow breaths.

Since that time, I've learned that deep breathing is an effective way to center yourself. It's a common meditation practice. Taking in deep breaths also aids your respiratory system.

UC Health shares that, "Respiratory muscles are working every minute of the day, every day of our lives." As a matter of fact, we take about 20,000 breaths each day.[1]

If you're like me, it might feel awkward to breathe deeply. However, it's a good habit to start and maintain. Why?

When you take deep, relaxing breaths, you "allow your body to fully exchange incoming oxygen with outgoing carbon dioxide," according to UC Health. Additional benefits you can feel when you breathe deeply include a lower heartbeat, more stabilized blood pressure and, of course, less stress.

As a tip, UC Health shares that, to breathe deeply in a healthy way, "Breathe slowly and deeply through your nose, causing your stomach to rise and expand. Exhale fully." Do this for several minutes. Try to make breathing deeply or more fully a normal part of your day.

Harvard Health Publishing recommends finding a quiet place to lay down and practice deep breathing. They suggest laying down, relaxing and focusing on deep breathing for 10 to 20 minutes each day.[2]

They also share that you could sit up and practice deep breathing. Start by taking normal breaths and then build up to deep breaths. Again, breath in through your nose and out through your mouth or nose, whichever feels more comfortable for you.

Focusing on a picture on the wall or focusing on a positive inner image that you create in your mind could aid you during the deep breathing process. The aim is to make taking deep breaths a part of your daily routine.

Of the many smart actions that you can take to improve your life, breathing deeply might be one of the easiest. It's definitely one of the top "free" ways to improve your life, physically and emotionally.

"The wisest one-word sentence? Breathe."
Terri Guillemets

Resources:
1. https://www.uchealth.org/today/understanding-breathing-and-the-importance-of-taking-a-deep-breath/
2. https://www.health.harvard.edu/mind-and-mood/relaxation-techniques-breath-control-helps-quell-errant-stress-response

Where's Your Favorite Place to Relax and Breathe Deeply?

_____

_____

_____

_____

_____

_____

_____

_____

_____

Week 50
What's Your Benefit

Relationships are the cornerstone of healthy lifestyles, be those relationships personal, social or business focused. Each time that you network, you demonstrate that you are willing to not only introduce yourself to new people but that you are also willing to deepen your existing relationships.

To be effective, it's important to approach networking with the mindset of sharing and helping others. If you attend networking events, again be those events personal, social or business focused, with the intent of only seeing what you can gain from people who attend networking events, you could walk away frustrated.

Another takeaway that you could leave with is a sense that networking doesn't work or that attending networking events isn't worth your time. So, attend networking events with the goal of offering benefit. For example, you could come prepared to share a valuable tip with each person you connect with at networking events.

This would allow you to offer an immediate benefit to others. Other ways to make networking valuable are to:

- Ask a friend, social contact or colleague to make a personal introduction to someone you want to connect with.
- Add contact details at your website to encourage customer interactions (apply cybersecurity protocols when adding contact details).
- Use social media to network online.
- Remember that each person offers infinite value.
- Exchange customized business cards (some networkers do expect you to be able to give them a business card).
- Offer dates and times for when you can follow-up with relevant contacts that you meet at networking events.
- Join social or hobby-related and professional organizations. Attend conferences, seminars, festivals and other networking events that these organizations host.
- Go to networking events that are attended by influencers and people you want to deepen connections with. In other words, don't just attend one major networking event that allows you to communicate with certain people, attend *several events* that put you in contact with these people.

- Respond to legitimate online and offline inquiries. Sometimes a response is one of the more effective ways to build relationship.
- Aim to build sincere relationships, including friendships, with people you network with. Genuinely care about people in your network.

Even if you lived on an island, you would enter relationships. There would be your relationships with the plant and animal life around you, not to mention your relationship to yourself. It's impossible to not be in a relationship.

Networking is a skill that, if practiced correctly, can lead to better relationships. While networking, you learn the art of active listening and how to sharpen communication skills. Side benefits include improved ability to read body language, decipher personal energy and know what to say (and not to say) and when.

"Personal relationships are always the key to good business. You can buy networking; you can't buy friendships."

Lindsay Fox

How Have You Made Networking Fun Over the Last 3 Months?

_____

_____

_____

_____

_____

_____

_____

_____

_____

_____

_____

Week 51
When You're Tempted to Quit

Life in this world doesn't come with a roadmap, at least not the type of map that you can see with your physical eyes. Even if you engage in daily spiritual practices, there are surprises, experiences that you just don't see coming.

Fortunately, many of these unforeseen experiences might very well be good. They also might get better and better. Howbeit, you may never know this if you don't keep going. It may help to revisit a time in your life when you almost quit, when you felt a strong urge to just "give up".

Imagine how it felt when you truly believed that there was no more good awaiting you. Experience what it felt like to take that next step. Recall how you felt when you entered a new, exciting and more rewarding phase. Continue to think about the fact that you didn't see that new good coming.

You also might find it helpful to be willing to relinquish control. There's simply too much that you don't know. For example, do you know how many lines are running horizontally and vertically across your hands? Do you know how many objects you've seen or touched this year? Can you count and describe them all?

What if your Source knows those answers?

Release the past. Take the lessons that you've gained and bring them forward with you. Be willing to be led by Love instead of fear. Despite how many years you've been having your physical experience, stay open. Expect better experiences to come to you.

Receive those new experiences with appreciation. Should you become discouraged, read motivational and inspirational books. Surround yourself with people who care about you and who will say and do things to encourage you and lift you up.

As previously mentioned throughout this book, be flexible, adaptable and willing to try new approaches. Not every door may open the first time that you knock on it. Additionally, you might have to use a different key to enter new experiences that you want to have.

Throughout your journey, be patient with yourself and others. If you got everything that you wanted right away, you could feel overwhelmed. Trust the universe's timing. Yet, don't be passive. Seek guidance, steer clear of magical thinking and take smart action.

Trust.

And remember, the only way to discover what will become of your entire physical experience is to keep going. You simply must continue to trust God and keep moving forward.

"As I look back on my life, I realized that every time I thought I was being rejected from something good, I was actually being re-directed to something better."
Anonymous

List 7 Smart Actions That You're Taking to Keep Moving in the Right Direction

_____

_____

_____

_____

_____

_____

_____

_____

_____

_____

_____

Week 52
Trust God

All of life may come down to this – trusting God.

The struggle is that experiences in this physical world can seemingly go completely counter to what you've been told to believe about God. You might say prayers that never seem to get answered. If you're like me, you might engage in spiritual practices like meditation, scripture reading, prayer, nature walks, drinking lots of fresh water and stillness only to be left wondering what to do next.

My writing journey has definitely been an exercise in trust. Successes that I have realized have come due to absolute refusal to quit, a willingness to take smart actions, continuing to learn, network and trust. Like you, I simply do not see all that is coming.

Because you have to make decisions that take in your physical experiences and what you pick up through your five senses, it could feel odd to trust in outcomes that don't rely on the body or its senses. For this reason, you might have to simply trust step-by-step.

As you continue to trust, you might become stronger in this area. Yet, you have to trust God at least once to get started. Looking back over your life, you might also discover that you have been trusting God and simply thought that you had merely been going with the flow.

Another point to reflect on is that there's direction and thoughts that derive from the ego as well as from God. This is where stillness, prayer, meditation and nature walks may help. During these times, simply let your mind rest and become quiet. For it's long been shared that it's into a quiet mind that the voice of God enters.

Keep going, inwardly seeing and believing in the best for you. Keep trusting God. You just might be surprised at how your life turns out as you continue your journey.

"Trust in the LORD with all your heart and lean not on your own understanding; in all your ways submit to him, and he will make your paths straight."
Proverbs 3:5-6

Which 4 Ways Have You Started to Trust God This Year?

_____

_____

_____

_____

_____

_____

_____

_____

_____

_____

_____

Thank you for reading <u>Pathways to Tremendous Success</u>. I encourage you to keep a blessings journal and track the results of your efforts. If this book blessed you in any way, please tell someone else about it. Also, become consistent in your efforts, committed to your life investments.

Stopping when you feel discouraged and starting when you feel inspired may not achieve the results you're looking for. So, practice faith, seek and accept inner guidance and keep advancing. You really can design an amazingly rewarding and beautiful life for yourself. It is within you to achieve that.

Should your aim be to achieve literary success, consider subscribing to The Book Lover's Haven newsletter for free at – <u>www.chistell.com</u>. Within the newsletter, you'll find information on job openings, writing events, literary entrepreneurs and more.

If you're seeking ongoing motivation and insight, consider listening to Off The Shelf - <u>https://www.blogtalkradio.com/denise-turney-</u>. There you will discover feature interviews with business owners, entrepreneurs, overcomers, movie producers, life coaches and artists.

SUCCESS DEVOTIONAL

Made in United States
Orlando, FL
14 June 2025

62102485R00138